Wr

Get **more** out of libraries

Please return or renew this item by the last date shown.

You can renew online at www.hants.gov.uk/library

Or by phoning 0300 555 1387

Hampshire
County Council

What would Nietzsche do?

How the greatest **philosophers** would solve your everyday problems

Marcus Weeks

CASSELL ILLUSTRATED

An Hachette UK Company
www.hachette.co.uk

First published in Great Britain in 2017 by Cassell, a division of
Octopus Publishing Group Ltd
Carmelite House
50 Victoria Embankment
London EC4Y 0DZ
www.octopusbooks.co.uk

ISBN 978 1 84403 926 5
A CIP catalogue record for this book is available from the British Library.

Printed and bound in China

10 9 8 7 6 5 4 3 2 1

Editorial Director: Trevor Davies
Senior Editor: Alex Stetter
Art Director: Yasia Williams
Designer: Ella McLean
Production Controller: Sarah Kulasek-Boyd

Contents

Introduction

We all need advice from time to time. Life has a habit of presenting us with dilemmas, some serious, some trivial, that require a bit of thought, and maybe some guidance. And when it comes to thinking through problems, there's nobody more skilled than the great philosophers. The trouble is, they were generally so preoccupied with thinking about the big stuff – life, the universe and everything – that they seldom gave us the benefit of their wisdom on the little things, the problems of everyday life.

So, we can't be sure exactly what any philosopher's answer would be, but we can get a pretty fair idea of the way each thinker would look at the problem. That's what this book is about. What would the great thinkers (not just Nietzsche, although his opinions crop up quite frequently) advise when faced with the practical problems of relationships, work, lifestyle, leisure and politics in the modern world? The sort of problems you might raise with your friends or family, or write to the agony aunt in a magazine about?

Now, these problems are not specifically "philosophical", but, like almost everything, they can be approached philosophically. So you might find that some philosophers would use the question as a springboard to jump off into deeper waters, exploring the hidden implications of a dilemma, and many of them would make the connection between the question and their own ideas and theories.

More often than not, there is no one solution to the problem, and different philosophers might give conflicting advice, reflecting the often contradictory nature of philosophy. The different attitudes of the philosophers to these problems not only present us with options when making a decision, but also gives an insight into some of the different approaches to philosophical problems. Some philosophers are more interested in a particular area of philosophy, such as ethics or logic, than others. As a result, certain philosophers appear more than others in different sections of the book. Marx, for instance, is more likely to have an opinion on politics than Kant, and Descartes is less interested in aesthetics than Aristotle. There are, however, some thinkers who are regular contributors to the discussions; the Athenians, Socrates, Plato and Aristotle, for example, generally have something to say about just about everything. There are others who are notable for their absence, simply because their philosophies are not relevant to the topics discussed – and in any case there is not room to include everybody!

From this panel of experts, we can benefit from a wide range of opinions, and enjoy

some lively debate. Several of the pundits
emerge as major players in these discussions,
representing some of the important strands
of philosophical thought. But this isn't a
textbook of philosophy, doesn't pretend
to present a comprehensive survey of
philosophy and can only introduce
some of the ideas through
their application to everyday
problems. You might also
discover that there is more
to philosophy than just the
ideas. As you consider the
arguments put forward by the
various thinkers, you will become
aware of their characters too: from
the intentionally irritating Socrates,
the idealistic Plato and prosaic
Aristotle to the mischievous
Machiavelli, po-faced Kant,
grumpy Schopenhauer,
iconoclastic Nietzsche and
many more. Some you will
warm to, and feel an affinity
with their advice; others will
be less attractive. You might
even find that you can enjoy
hearing their different
points of view without
necessarily agreeing with
their ideas, or conversely
that you find their
arguments persuasive without
warming to their personalities.
That's philosophy for you.

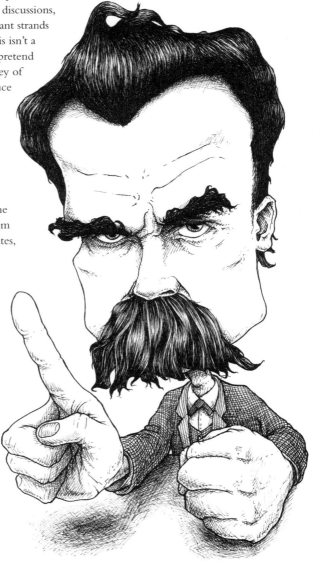

Relationships

Chapter 1

My friend's partner is cheating on her – should I tell her?

Kant • Bentham

You really are facing a dilemma here. Your friend is blissfully unaware of her partner's philandering, and you don't know whether to shatter her illusions. Of course, you'd feel terrible about telling her an outright lie, but it's just as uncomfortable for you to keep something from her. Somehow you feel a duty to be honest with her, but you know the pain that will cause, and you can't be sure how she'll react. It seems you're damned if you do, and damned if you don't – and whatever you decide, you want her to know that you did it with the best of intentions.

Looking for guidance on this from the philosophers takes us into some very deep waters, to the fundamental questions of how we judge what is morally right or wrong. So don't expect any easy answers.

You've probably been brought up, like most people, to believe that lying is wrong, plain and simple. You should always tell the truth. It couldn't be clearer than that, could it? This is the view known in philosophy as *deontology*, that there are moral rules that are absolute, and we have a duty to follow them. If you break the rule, your action is morally wrong. The best-known advocate of this approach to morality was **Immanuel Kant** (1724–1804), who summed the idea up in

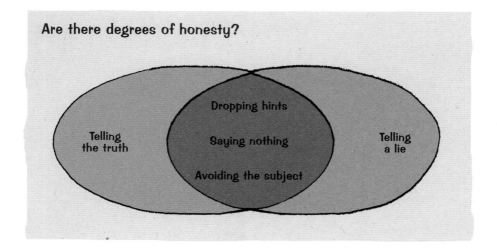

Are there degrees of honesty?

Telling the truth

Dropping hints

Saying nothing

Avoiding the subject

Telling a lie

what he called the "categorical imperative": act only in accordance with a maxim that you can at the same time will to become a universal law. Which means that if you think something, lying for example, is generally wrong, then it is always wrong, without exception, no matter what.

This black and white approach seems pretty straightforward, but aren't there perhaps some grey areas too? If your friend asks you outright if her partner is cheating, you have a moral duty to tell her the truth. But if she doesn't...you're not actually lying, but not actually telling the truth either. Or maybe the moral law is that it's wrong to hide the truth, or that you should always tell everybody everything. What, even things that are completely irrelevant to them?

Truth and consequences

Following moral rules is not necessarily the simple solution to this dilemma that it seems, so you might want to consider a completely different approach, *consequentialism*, which judges the moral rightness or wrongness of an action by its outcomes. It's the basis of much of moral philosophy since the Renaissance, in contrast to the especially religious "commandments" of what is right or wrong. Particularly relevant to the

> ### Basic philosophical question
>
> Do we have a moral duty to always tell the truth, or is it sometimes morally justifiable to leave it unsaid, conceal it or even tell a lie?

problem of to tell or not to tell is **Jeremy Bentham's** (1748–1832) idea of assessing the "utility" of an action, weighing up the amount of happiness or harm it creates. In your case, you would consider all the possible outcomes of telling your friend, or not telling her, and base your decision on how much good or harm it will cause, both immediately and in the long term. You might then decide to withhold the information, or even tell a "white lie", to protect her, and still feel justified in tearing up the moral rulebook; or, rather than see her live a lie, to be the bearer of hurtful tidings, but ultimately in her best interests.

And here, you'll start to see that we're thinking not just about outcomes, but also about your own intentions and motives

"The truth, the whole truth and nothing but the truth"
From the oath or affirmation of a witness in court
to give sworn testimony

> *"I ought never to act except in such a way that I could also will that my maxim should become a universal law"*
> Immanuel Kant

for what you do. This is part of the area of philosophy known as *virtue ethics*, which, like consequentialism, considers morality on a case-by-case basis, but, instead of concentrating on individual actions, examines the "virtue" of the person taking them. So, rather than saying that it is morally right or wrong to do something, we look at the reasons for making that decision, whether the person making the decision is acting in their own interests or those of others, for instance, and this is dependent on their own inner sense of morality. So, if you do something because you honestly believe it is the right thing to do in the circumstances, you are acting morally, even if you tell a lie, and even if it all goes horribly wrong. The mere fact that you agonize over what to do, whatever you eventually decide, is a mark of your personal morality.

Making a decision

You may think, like Kant, that you have a duty to be honest with your friend, even if it is painful. But then, are you being entirely honest if you just avoid telling her? Bentham urges you to look at the likely consequences of telling her, or not telling her. Perhaps she would prefer to know what's going on.

How do I mend a broken heart?

Boethius • de Beauvoir • Epicurus • Zeno of Citium • Buddha • Schopenhauer • Nietzsche

You're in a bad place right now. The person you cared about more than anything else in the world has left you. Of course, the world hasn't come to an end – it just seems that way. Nothing else matters. You don't want to feel so down, but you can't see an end to the misery, or any point in trying to get over it. To be honest, you can't see the point in anything at the moment. How are you supposed to get on with your life when your whole world has been shattered? And what's the point of all the pain you're going through right now?

Well, this is a serious problem. Not a matter of life or death, maybe, especially when looked at from the outside, but for the person going through it, it can seem that way. It's a universal experience too, so you'd expect most philosophers to have some good advice on the subject. The Roman thinker **Boethius** (*c.*480–524) wrote a book titled *The Consolation of Philosophy*, giving us hope that philosophers might have some pointers, but it turns out he just recommends turning your mind to higher things. And, just as they do on almost every other subject,

philosophers have some widely differing opinions on dealing with a broken heart. These can be divided into three main camps: the "snap out of it and get on with life", the "grin and bear it" and the "this will make you a better person".

A good person to turn to for guidance, particularly if you're a woman, might be the French philosopher **Simone de Beauvoir** (1908–86). As well as being a straightforward, no-nonsense feminist, and a down-to-earth *existentialist*, she had plenty of personal experience in matters of the heart, or at least the bedroom. Unusually for a woman of her time, the mid-20th century, she had the "love 'em and leave 'em" attitude more common among macho men, and would probably tell you that there are plenty more fish in the sea. Not that that helps at all when you're wallowing in self-pity, of course. But she wouldn't leave it at that. Long before the slogan "the personal is political" became the rallying cry of second-wave feminism, de Beauvoir was preaching the message and living the life. What's sauce for the gander, she said, is sauce for the goose: why should

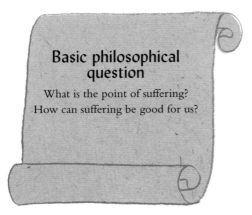

Basic philosophical question

What is the point of suffering? How can suffering be good for us?

women be bound by conventions of femininity?

So, you shouldn't expect too much sympathy from her. She would more likely tell you to get a grip and take control of the situation, instead of letting it control you. Male or female, she'd get you thinking about how you let yourself get into this miserable state. You made a romantic relationship the main source of meaning in your life, and now it's gone...what do you expect? There are other things in life, just as important, and you have the choice to pursue them. In the end, it's up to you to make your own happiness or misery, and not rely on other people to provide you with a purpose. Simply put, she'd tell you to get over it, and make sure you don't get hurt again. Her advice is rather like locking the stable door

after the horse has bolted, though, and might seem a bit harsh while you're nursing your wounds. You want to know what to do now to go about treating them.

The Greek philosopher **Epicurus** (341–270 BCE), a couple of thousand years de Beauvoir's senior, might broadly agree with her. His guiding principle was to minimize pain (not, as is popularly thought, simply to seek pleasure), so he wouldn't have much sympathy with you for bringing all that suffering on yourself. But, rather than dwelling on it and prolonging the agony, he'd recommend finding ways to ease the pain, and in particular calming the desires that got you into the mess in the first place. Then you can start looking for things that genuinely give you pleasure, and know how to avoid those that will hurt you.

Get over it

Well meaning though Epicurus's advice might be, it probably won't help you much in coming to terms with your current situation. If you're looking for more practical ways of getting through it, maybe one of the Stoics could help. Another Greek, **Zeno of Citium** (c.334–262 BCE), the founder of the Stoic school of philosophy, reckoned he had the answer to achieving peace of mind, so he might be a good choice. He was, however, realistic and virtuous to the point of being stern and austere – so his advice might be a bit hard to swallow. He would

"There is nothing more whole than a broken heart"
Attributed to Rabbi Menachem Mendel of Kotzk, the "Kotzker Rebbe"

tell you that the way to get through life is to live in harmony with nature, and that means come rain or come shine. You mustn't let the bad stuff get you down, nor get over-excited by the good stuff. And, above all, you'll just get frustrated and upset if you try to change things that you have no control over.

If you're angling for sympathy, though, you might be better off looking for it from a more spiritual source. **Buddha** (born *c.*6th–4th century BCE), for example. He even looks more sympathetic, with that beatific smile. And, yes, he would sympathize; he was only too aware that the world is full of suffering, but he knew a way to get over it. He would tell you he knows how awful it is, all that suffering, but that it comes from having desires that cannot be satisfied. Yes, you've lost the love of your life, but, even if you still had it, you wouldn't be content. If you want an end to the suffering, you must stop getting attached to stuff and people. He would then pitch his "eightfold path" – the Buddhist guide to good living – that could help you overcome the insatiable desires causing your misery. Stick with the programme, and you could achieve eternal tranquillity.

Long before it became fashionable with hippies in the West, the German philosopher **Arthur Schopenhauer** (1788–1860) was fascinated by Indian philosophy, and borrowed from it to form his own world view. But, unless you want just to wallow in your despondency, he's maybe not a great person to turn to. He was quite possibly the gloomiest, most pessimistic philosopher of all time, and was bad-tempered with it. Like Buddha, he recognized that there is suffering everywhere, all the time, but he would make a point of telling you that there is no way of avoiding that. You're trying to mend a broken heart? Don't bother. The world is full of misery, and there's nothing you can do about it, except maybe lose yourself in philosophy or music. Whatever you do, it will all end in tears. Get used to it – it's the human condition.

A positive experience

Perhaps the most optimistic advice you could get would be from **Friedrich Nietzsche** (1844–1900). Having been through the horrible early death of his father, a crisis of faith and the rejection of his lover, he knew

Schopenhauer

> *"What does not destroy me, makes me stronger"*
> Friedrich Nietzsche

only too well what it's like to be heart-broken. Despite these tragedies, he found a way to turn them into a positive philosophy. Where many philosophers with a religious conviction would turn to their faith for comfort, Nietzsche rejected the idea that we should accept that suffering is somehow part of God's purpose for us. Instead, he'd agree with Schopenhauer that we're doomed to some misery in our lives, but that we should look on this as an opportunity rather than a setback. He would sympathize with you to a certain extent, and let you know that your suffering is an inevitable part of being human. But he would advise you not just to get over the suffering, but to find meaning in it. In his experience, he would say, the pain is necessary and can be life-affirming. The things we strive to do, if they are worth doing, involve the risk of failure, and the suffering that they bring helps us to appreciate our achievements all the more. If we approach with it with the right attitude, every period of suffering in life serves to make us stronger, more able to live the life we want to lead. Just don't look at his biography, though, as you'll find out that he never really got over being turned down by his sweetheart, and died a broken man, aged 55, insane and syphilitic.

Making a decision

Do you think de Beauvoir has the right idea, that to get over the break-up, you should just forget about it and get on with your life? Or are you more inclined to believe Zeno, Buddha and Schopenhauer when they tell you that, if you really must fall in love, you have to accept the inevitability of pain and suffering? And if you have to go through the misery of heartbreak, do you think Nietzsche has a point about learning something from the experience that will help you in the future and maybe enrich your life?

I'm having a silent battle with my partner about the setting of the thermostat for our heating.

Protagoras • Plato • Berlin

You like to keep the house at a nice even temperature, let's say about 20°C (68°F). But you keep finding that, especially when it's getting colder outside, the thermostat has been changed to something more like 25°C (77°F). Although nothing is said, you know your partner is sneakily turning it up, even though you keep putting it back to the right level. Meanwhile, the kids are saying that your preferred temperature is unnaturally warm, and tell you to put more clothes on to save the planet. You're pretty sure that there is a "Goldilocks" temperature, though, not too hot, not too cold. About 20°C (68°F), in fact.

This is one of those debates that's going to run and run. You have a point of view, that a comfortable temperature for your house is about 20°C (68°F), but your family disagree. Your partner thinks that's a bit chilly, while your children think it's unnecessarily warm. You can argue until you're blue in the face, but they aren't going to change their minds. You can't all be right, can you?

Actually, **Protagoras** (*c.*490–420 BCE) would say that maybe you can. He'd point out that your opinion is just that, a point of view, and that it is valid for you. It's how you perceive things from your perspective. But then you'll have to concede that your partner is entitled to an opinion too. 20°C (68°F) is, from your partner's perspective, just not warm enough to be comfortable. And who are you to say that's wrong? Isn't that point of view equally valid?

Ah yes, you might reply, you'd be willing to accept that if it were a consistent stance, but

your partner would have the house hotter in the winter than it is during the summer. And come the spring, you go out for a walk together, and you both agree how pleasantly warm it is in the sunshine. And it's about 20°C (68°F), for pete's sake!

You're missing the point, Protagoras would argue. It doesn't matter whether your partner's opinion is consistent or not. It's about his perception of the heat or cold, not the actual temperature in degrees. Protagoras could give a couple of examples to make the point a bit clearer. Take when you went on that holiday to Egypt to see the Pyramids. It was really hot, remember? Uncomfortably hot. Even after two weeks, you found it difficult to acclimatize. But when you got home, even though the weather was mild, it felt chilly. It's all relative, you see. It wasn't cold according to any absolute measure of the temperature, but relative to the heat in Cairo, it felt chilly. From your perspective.

> *"Absolute relativism, which is neither more nor less than skepticism, in the most modern sense of the term, is the supreme triumph of the reasoning reason"*
> Miguel de Unamuno

Another example: you're enjoying a pleasant afternoon in the sunshine in Los Angeles – it's about 20°C (68°F), just how you like it – when you meet up with some visitors to the city. The Alaskan family are in shorts and T-shirts, searching for a bit of shade, while the Iraqi family huddle together in their coats and scarves (your kids would say they've got the right idea about how to keep warm).

You can't tell them they're wrong to feel the cold or the heat: they just do. They each have, as do you, a valid point of view. And Protagoras would say that a lot of other things are relative too, that there isn't necessarily a right or wrong answer and that people are entitled to have different points of view about matters of taste and feelings,

and also about questions of morality. Your opinion, your point of view, is bound to be influenced by where you come from, just like the visitors to LA.

So, while you might find eating pork and drinking alcohol quite normal, for example, someone from a strict Islamic culture would find it unacceptable. And although you're outraged by the barbarism of bullfighting, it's considered by some to be an art form. Your ideas of what is normal and acceptable – from whether you prefer spicy or bland food to your opinions on the death penalty – depend on the culture you come from.

Protagoras made a living from pleading cases in the ancient Greek courts and, like all lawyers, no doubt often argued for things he himself didn't believe in. So when he

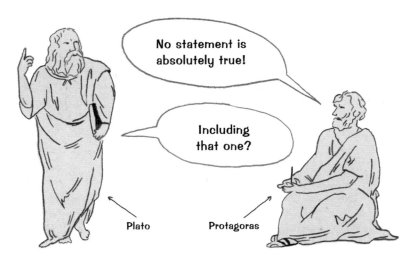

Plato — No statement is absolutely true!

Protagoras — Including that one?

> *"A writer who says that there are no truths, or that all truth is 'merely relative', is asking you not to believe him. So don't"*
> Roger Scruton

said that there are always two sides to an argument, you might want to take that with a hefty dose of salt – it was just a bit of rhetoric to get his point about *relativism* across. There are, he would admit, some things that are just plain wrong. All the same, a lot of people have taken him at his word, and relativism, especially *cultural relativism*, has become a benchmark of a tolerant, liberal society – to the extent that overenthusiastic adherence to political correctness forbids any criticism of some pretty dubious practices, such as female genital mutilation. Protagoras would, however, warn against trying to take the moral high ground and saying that some things are self-evidently wrong, quietly pointing out that until shamefully recently, US and European cultures found it quite acceptable to run a slave trade and employ child labour.

Basic philosophical question

Can a point of view have absolute truth or validity? Or is it relative – dependent on our subjective perception and judgement? Do ideas of what is right and wrong depend on who you are and the environment you live in?

It's all relative

It would seem to be quite difficult to argue against relativism then, and it looks like you're not going to win the battle of the thermostat. There are, however, degrees of relativism. Protagoras puts up a convincing case against *absolutism*, the view that nothing is relative, that it's not about subjective points of view and that there is always a right or wrong answer. At the other extreme, however, there are the strong, radical relativists who would insist that everything is relative – even if that means having to accept some morally repugnant opinions as valid points of view.

It's here that **Plato** (*c.*427–347 BCE) could come to your rescue. He didn't buy Protagoras's arguments at all, and saw them as a cheap lawyer's trick to shrug off responsibility. But he found a logical flaw in the fundamental claim of relativism. If you assert that every point of view is relative and therefore valid, then you are undermining your own case. Your own point of view, that everything is relative, is just a point of view which is true for you – and my point of view, that everything is not relative, which is true for me, is equally valid. The arguments of the radical relativist are exposed as self-contradictory.

Most people, however, would go along with the idea that there are some things that are either right or wrong, true or false, and others that are a matter of perspective. But it's not easy to justify that sort of middle ground. Unless you're **Isaiah Berlin** (1909–97),

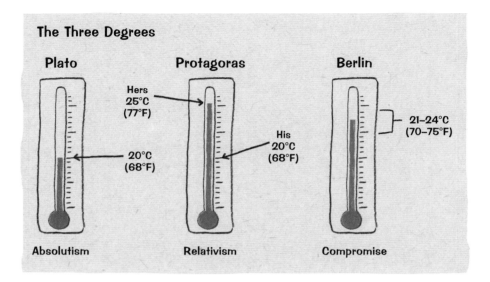

The Three Degrees

Plato — Absolutism

Protagoras — Relativism

Hers 25°C (77°F)

His 20°C (68°F)

20°C (68°F)

Berlin — Compromise

21–24°C (70–75°F)

of course. His reading of the problem is a common-sense one, that neither absolutism nor strict relativism hold water. Instead, he said that, although there are no absolutes in matters of taste or morality or judgement, if you look around you'll find that most people in every different culture have values and opinions in common, such as that lying, stealing, murder and so on are wrong, and that liberty, justice and so on are good. These values are universal, and only differ in detail or practice.

Now then, your position on the thermostat is one of an absolutist: there is

an ideal temperature, it's not a question of perspective, and either you or your partner is right. But your partner's stance is that of a relativist: some people feel the cold more than others, it's not a question of right and wrong. Perhaps you could come to some sort of compromise, along the lines of Berlin's argument. Although there may be minor differences of opinion (a matter of a few degrees, that's all), there will be some consensus on roughly what is an acceptable temperature, or at least an acceptable temperature range. Live with it.

Making a decision

It depends if you're willing to accept Protagoras's idea that your opinion and your partner's are both valid. If you do, then you'll have to find a compromise, as Berlin suggests. Otherwise, either you or your partner will have to find a convincing argument, or continue the battle.

I just found out that my dad is not my dad!

Socrates • Aristotle • Gettier • James

Your world turns upside down when something you thought you knew turns out not to be the case. It makes you wonder if you can ever really know anything for certain. But sometimes you have to accept something as the truth. But does this new knowledge negate what you believed to be true? Perhaps believing he was your dad was "true enough" for you at the time, and it's only now that you have to change your ideas about what you know. It could be that there are different degrees of "truth", and that your perception of what is true changes as you discover more facts.

If you thought that it was tough coming to terms with the news that your dad isn't who you thought he was, be warned that philosophy isn't going to make it any easier. No matter which philosopher you turn to, they're going to be more interested in what you know, or think you know, than how you feel about it. What you're looking for here is to make some sense of the situation. And that isn't all that simple.

The whole thing turns on what you know, and what you thought that you knew. So,

Basic philosophical question

What is knowledge? How do I actually know anything? What is truth? Does it matter if what I believe I know is true, so long as it is useful?

the philosopher of choice here is **Socrates** (*c.*469–399 BCE), who was declared by none other than the Oracle at Delphi to be the wisest person in Athens. Because he knew nothing. But, more importantly, because he knew that he knew nothing. So, instead of going around telling everybody what he knew, he went around asking them what they knew. And then he asked them how they knew that they knew what they thought they knew (you were warned that this isn't going to be easy). And what made them think that it was true, whether it was just a belief, or whether they really knew it.

By this persistent and undoubtedly annoying questioning, which was later made respectable as the "Socratic method" of *dialectical reasoning*, Socrates chipped away at assumptions and conventions, leading people on to contradict themselves and end up doubting just about everything they thought they believed in. But he wasn't simply point-scoring, showing how clever he was at the "yes but" game. He really was wiser than he let on, and by exposing the fallacies we all go along with, tried to get to the nub of concepts such as "knowledge " and "truth".

What's that got to do with your dad? Well, Socrates would ask you (he wouldn't tell you anything, remember) if, before you got the news, you knew that he was your dad. And then how you knew that. And then, what you know now, and how you know that, and so on. Now, that's all very well, but it doesn't help you to come to terms with the revelation about your dad (or not-dad). Actually, you will probably just get to the state where you don't know what you do know, or whether anything you thought you knew is true. Socrates's student **Plato** would probably tell you, on the quiet, that all his teacher's questioning drove him slightly mad too, and that he'd recommend you just accept that there is always a real possibility that your beliefs are false. But Plato's student **Aristotle** (384–322 BCE) wouldn't let go that easily...

Unlike Plato, who was a bit of a dreamer, Aristotle was systematic and methodical to the point of being obsessive. So he wouldn't be satisfied with just saying that what you believe may be false. He wanted to pin down what it means to know something, so that we can apply that in the real world. And he came up with a pretty good definition of knowledge as "justified true belief". For example, he would ask you if you know

> I'm an Athenian.

> How do you know?

> My dad told me.

> Does he always tell the truth?

> No, I suppose not, but...

where you were born. Yes, you reply, I know I was born in Athens. So, obviously, you believe that, but he'd ask whether you had anything to back up your claim. Yes, here's a birth certificate. So your belief is justified. And, when he checks with the midwife, he finds it's true. So, because it's a justified and true belief, you're right to say you know.

Getting back to your dad, Aristotle would

> *"Nothing is so firmly believed as what is least known"*
> Michel de Montaigne

ask if you believed he was your dad. Yes, because everybody told you that he was. Aha! So your belief was justified. But, as it turns out, he isn't your dad, so the belief was not true. And that means you didn't actually *know* he was your dad. Oh yes, you say – I knew he was hiding something from me. But did you? You might have believed he was, and as it happens that is true, but you had no justification for that belief. So, again, you didn't *know* he was deceiving you. And now, you've been told he isn't your dad. Think about it: do you know he isn't your dad? Do you believe he isn't? Is there any evidence to suggest he isn't? Is it true?

True enough

The "justified true belief" (JTB) definition is a good way of testing whether you really know something, but it's not infallible. If you were to ask **Edmund L. Gettier III** (b. 1927), he'd throw a spanner in the JTB works. You tell him you got the results of DNA tests, which show that the person you thought was your dad is not your dad. So now you know. But do you? Gettier then explains that there was a mix-up at the lab, and they sent you someone else's results. But the correct results (although you don't know this, yet) do show that he isn't your dad. Your belief that he isn't your dad happens

to be true, and you are justified in believing it, because you had the letter. But you can't really say that you "know" that it's true, because your knowledge of the truth is based on false evidence.

So, even when you thought you had proof that your justified belief was true, you didn't really *know*. But does it really matter? You know now. As far as you know, anyway. Before you had the bombshell about him not being your dad, though, you thought you knew he was your dad. But the point is, you didn't know that you didn't know. Donald Rumsfeld, one-time US Secretary of Defense, was widely (and unjustly) mocked for explaining this situation: "...as we know, there are known knowns; there are things we know we know. We also know there are known unknowns; that is to say we know there are some things we do not know. But there are also unknown unknowns – the ones we don't know we don't know." You believed he was your dad, and while it may not have actually been true, it was true for you. And, until you found out the facts, it was "true enough" for your purposes.

That might sound like a bit of a cop-out, but it's probably going to help you understand and deal with your confusion about your parentage a lot better than all the abstract musing about "knowledge" and

> "To say of what is, that it is, or of what is not, that it is not, is true"
> Aristotle

> *"If you would be a real seeker after truth, you must at least once in your life doubt, as far as possible, all things"*
> René Descartes

"truth" and what they mean. And the idea of ditching the abstractions in favour of something that actually helps comes with pretty good credentials. **William James** (1842–1910) was a physician and a pioneer in the science of psychology, as well as being a highly respected American philosopher. Just the sort of person to give you some practical advice, then. In fact, he subscribed to the school of philosophy known as *pragmatism* which, put simply, couldn't see the point of any philosophy unless it had a practical application.

James would tell you that all that debate about what you actually know or don't know is a bit like trying to knit fog. And about as useful. It doesn't matter if you can't prove that you know something, it only matters how useful having that belief is to you. As James would explain it, if you believe something, and it is useful, then for you it is a "true belief". Take your dad, for example. You used to believe that he was your dad.

OK, it may not have actually been true, but it was true for you. Because you believed it was true, you could use it as a basis for other beliefs and ideas about yourself and your relationship with "your dad". You used that belief to make sense of things, so it was useful to you to believe it. According to James's definition, then, it was a true belief. And (this is a bit tricky to get your head round, but worth the effort) because it was a useful belief, it became the truth for you. It matched the facts as you knew them, and became the basis for other truths. Now facts are facts, and they don't change, but new facts may be revealed to you, which can make you change your beliefs, and that of course will mean you have a new truth, different from, but not better or worse than, your previous true belief. The truth changes, but the facts remain the same. The truth is, you believed he was your dad, but now don't believe that; the fact is, he never was your dad.

Making a decision

Coming to terms with this new information will make you question more than your parentage. You could follow Socrates and Aristotle and ask just what knowledge and truth really mean, and whether we can actually know what is true. Or you could go along with James, that the "truth" can change as new facts become available.

I ran over my neighbour's dog, avoiding another car...should I feel guilty?

Kant • Bentham • Thomas Aquinas • Foot

You must feel dreadful about that. There was really nothing else you could have done – the other car was headed straight at you, and neither of you could have braked in time, so you swerved onto the footpath where the dog was sitting. Of course you didn't mean to kill the poor animal, but you can't help feeling responsible for its death. It could have been so much worse, though, if you hadn't reacted so quickly. A head-on collision with a car full of people...how would you have felt about that? It doesn't bear thinking about.

The trouble is, though, that because you inevitably feel bad about running over your neighbour's dog, you are thinking about it. There's no getting away from the fact that it was your car, with you at the wheel, that caused the dog's death. And to that extent, you are responsible, but you shouldn't really feel guilty unless you've done something morally wrong, should you? So, the question here isn't whether you should feel guilty, but whether you have anything to feel guilty about.

And that depends on how much you want to beat yourself up about it. In typically stern fashion, **Immanuel Kant** would tell you that you've got good reason to feel guilty. You obviously think it's wrong to cause unnecessary suffering to animals, or you wouldn't be worrying about the incident. And if you believe that, then you ought to act according to the rule that it's always wrong to harm animals. So, no matter what the circumstances, it was wrong to run over the dog. OK, you probably didn't have much of a choice, and whatever you did would have been wrong, but it doesn't make what you did right.

What's more, Kant would tell you, piling on the guilt, you broke one of his cardinal rules: it's wrong to treat people as a means rather than an end. You treated the dog's life

Basic philosophical question

Is it morally wrong to do something bad if the result is for the greater good? Is it wrong to let something bad happen if you could have prevented it? Can an action be morally justifiable if the intentions are good?

as a means to an end, killing it in order to avoid a crash. Does it matter that it was a dog, not a person? Not really, because you have also caused your neighbour and her family distress and misery by your actions, so you have treated them as a means to an end. And what if it had been your neighbour rather than her dog on the footpath?

The least harm

Kant's stance probably sounds a bit harsh, particularly if you're trying to find a way of justifying your actions rather than a reason to put on the sackcloth and ashes. He talks about ends and means as if the consequences are irrelevant, but you took the action you did because you thought it was the best thing to do, that the outcome was the lesser of two evils. You weighed up, however fleetingly, the consequences and opted for the one that caused the least harm. That's a classic *utilitarian* approach, such as advocated by **Jeremy Bentham**, and he would say that, in the circumstances, you have nothing to reproach yourself for. You had a choice: run over the dog, or drive straight into

"In principle and in practice, in a right track and in a wrong one, the rarest of all human qualities is consistency"
Jeremy Bentham

"Act in such a way that you treat humanity, whether in your own person or in the person of any other, never merely as a means to an end, but always at the same time as an end"

Kant

The runaway train

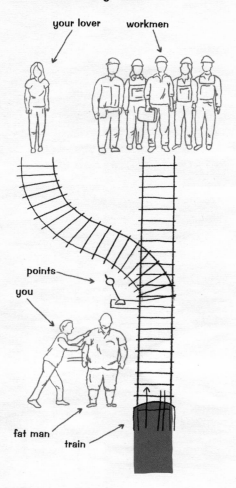

The train is hurtling towards five men working on the track. Only you can save them. Do you switch the points and kill your lover? Or do you push the fat man into the train's path to stop it? Or do you just let fate take its course?

> *"Morality is not properly the doctrine of how we may make ourselves happy, but how we may make ourselves worthy of happiness"*
> Immanuel Kant

an oncoming vehicle full of people; the probable death of one animal, compared with the possible death of several people (perhaps including yourself). You had to make an instant decision, and chose the right option.

That's one of the problems with utilitarianism, though. It seems a simple matter of doing what causes least harm, or most good. But you often don't have the time, or the information, to weigh up all the possible consequences. If you didn't have to react quickly to avoid a collision, you might have taken some other things into consideration. Maybe the death of a beloved pet would cause untold misery to an entire family, while if both vehicles braked and took evasive action the crash could have resulted in just a few minor injuries.

You meant well, though. It's a shame that the dog died, but that was not your intention, it was just "collateral damage", a necessary consequence of your action to avoid a major pile-up. And it's the intention that counts, right? **Thomas Aquinas** (*c.*1225–74) would go along with that. As a Christian, he would be concerned about whether actions are sinful or not, as they could condemn you to eternal damnation, not just pangs of guilt. For him, intention is everything. If you do something with good intentions, even if it has evil consequences, you have done nothing morally wrong. On the other hand, if your intentions are bad, no matter how well things turn out, you are a wicked sinner.

Things get a bit more complicated in a situation with a "double effect", particularly if you can foresee the outcomes, and you know that what you're doing will have both good and bad consequences. Then if your intention is to achieve something good, you can be forgiven for any less serious evil effects.

Good intentions

Take your case, for example. The double effect is that there was no car crash, but the dog got run over. What was your intention? To prevent harm to the occupants of the other car. Did you see the dog? If you didn't, then you couldn't have foreseen its death, and of course you didn't intend to kill it. But if you did see it, you must have foreseen that swerving towards it would almost certainly kill it. The death of the dog was an unintended, but foreseen, consequence. Let's say that the dog's owner subsequently commits suicide as a result of the distress caused by the loss of her companion. Although you would feel dreadful about it, you don't have any cause to feel guilt, as it's an effect that was neither intended nor foreseen. That last scenario might make you doubt the validity of the utilitarian idea of choosing the greatest good (or least harm) for the greatest number. How can you weigh up the consequences when you don't know what they will be?

Philippa Foot (1920–2010) would

29

suggest that there are other factors that complicate our judgement of what is right and wrong in situations like this; that we instinctively feel there's something dubious about doing something bad, even if the outcome is good and we do it with the best of intentions. She would also ask if it's only wrong to do something wrong, or if it's also wrong to do nothing to prevent something bad from happening.

To look at the rights and wrongs of the incident of the dog on the footpath, she'd present an analogous situation, a runaway train carriage hurtling down a track on which there are five workmen carrying out repairs. If it carries on, they'll certainly all be killed. You, however, can do something to prevent the tragedy, as she has put you in charge of the points between the carriage and the workmen, and you can divert it onto another track. Unfortunately, there's someone working on that track too, but just one man. If you weren't there, of course, he'd survive, and the five would be killed. Do you just let fate take its course, or do you switch the points and kill the single workman rather than the gang?

Now, what if it wasn't a single workman on the second track, but someone you knew or loved or someone who was conspicuously good? Would that influence your decision? Should it?

There is another way to stop the runaway carriage, however, but you're not going to like it. There's an enormously fat man standing by the track. If you pushed him in front of the carriage, his sheer bulk would stop it. He'd be killed, of course, but that's no worse than diverting the carriage toward the single workman. Or is it? Most of us balk at the thought of throwing someone in the path of an oncoming train, but wouldn't hesitate to pull the lever and send it down to kill some innocent workman. Kant would say that that's because you are forcibly confronted with the reality that you are treating the fat man as a means to an end. And perhaps he's got a point, after all.

Making a decision

Kant might explain your feeling guilty because you killed the dog as a means of avoiding an accident, and although this was probably the right thing to do, it cannot be morally justified. But you may argue, as Bentham would, that your actions prevented an even worse outcome, that it was the lesser of two evils, or use Aquinas's argument that you did it with good intentions.

My boyfriend spends most of his time playing computer games or on social media.

Epicurus • Bentham • Nozick • Putnam • Zhuangzi • Plato

This is really affecting your relationship, isn't it? It's got to the stage where there's almost no communication between the two of you, because he spends every waking moment either sitting at his computer or games console, or with his head bowed over his smartphone. He seems to be in a different world, a world of virtual reality, and he seems to prefer it to reality. You sometimes think that he believes that the world of gaming, avatars, video and chat rooms is the real world. And that the real world, the one you live in, is a poor substitute.

Now, what makes your boyfriend do that? The obvious answer is that he enjoys it, it gives him pleasure. Looking at it from another perspective, however, it could be that he's avoiding the real world, perhaps because he finds it difficult to deal with, or because it just seems dull. Or maybe he's immersing himself in that simulated reality because it gives him things he doesn't, or can't, get from the real world, things such as excitement, laughter and perhaps even companionship.

That's understandable, and to some extent forgivable. A number of philosophers, from **Epicurus** through to utilitarians such as **Jeremy Bentham**, would say that it's natural for us to seek pleasure and avoid pain, which is exactly what your boyfriend is doing. There's nothing intrinsically wrong with a bit of escapism, either getting away from the harsh realities of life, or relieving the boredom. After all, is his enjoyment of virtual reality any different, really, from watching TV, going to the cinema or even losing yourself in a good book? And, given the choice, don't we all want to do that?

It's a question of degree, though. Yes, we all choose to escape from time to time, to an imaginary world where we can enjoy the thrills, romance and so on that are missing from our real lives. Temporarily, we can decide to suspend our disbelief and experience a fantasy as if it were real.

> *"Only the refusal to listen guarantees one against being ensnared by the truth"*
> Robert Nozick

> *"No sane person should believe that something is 'subjective' merely because it cannot be settled beyond controversy"*
> Hilary Putnam

But would we really prefer those fictional experiences to the real thing? And would we choose to live permanently in a world of illusions?

Virtual reality

To help you answer that question, **Robert Nozick** (1938–2002) would invite you to imagine a machine he has invented, the "experience machine", the ultimate in virtual reality computers. When you switch it on, you don't have to suspend your disbelief, because it is linked directly to your brain and sends signals that stimulate the synapses and induce experiences that are indistinguishable from reality. You can programme the experience machine to give you all sorts of physical, mental and emotional sensations so real that you truly believe you are experiencing them. Of course, you can (and why wouldn't you?) choose to have pleasurable experiences, including some that you have never had before, or even imagined having. What's not to like?

But Nozick would ask you to think carefully about whether you'd really want to be hooked up to his experience machine. He asks if we really believe the idea that seeking pleasure (and avoiding pain) are our only values. If they are, then there's no reason not to plug in and turn on, because we'd get more pleasure that way than from living in the real world. Think again, though, and you might hesitate. Using the experience machine is a pretty passive business: you're not actually doing something, but having it done to you. And a lot of the things we want to do in life are because we want to actually *do* them, not just have the experience of doing them. And perhaps most importantly, even though the sensation is indistinguishable from reality, we know before we turn on the machine that what we're going to experience is not real.

So Nozick believes that we would not choose to be deceived by that sort of simulated reality. Most people would instinctively like to agree with him, too, preferring real experiences to virtual ones, but your boyfriend appears to be proving him wrong. Along with an increasing number of people who spend more time watching their phones than the world around them.

Nozick's experience machine is similar to an idea that **Hilary Putnam** (1926–2016) proposed, making us think about what we believe is reality actually is. Putnam's simulated

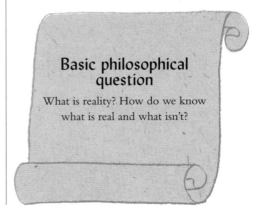

Basic philosophical question

What is reality? How do we know what is real and what isn't?

"Now I do not know whether I was then a man dreaming I was a butterfly, or whether I am now a butterfly dreaming I am a man."

Zhuangzi

reality is, however, rather more sinister. Imagine, he says, that there is an evil scientist who has removed someone's brain from their body and is keeping it alive in a vat of essential fluids. He's devised a method of connecting all the brain cells to a computer (just like Nozick's machine) that can stimulate the nerve endings so that the brain experiences things as if they were real. In his madness, the scientist programmes the computer to deceive the brain into thinking that it is not in a vat at all, but in its original body, and able to experience the world around it. But of course these experiences are illusory, and just the result of electronic stimuli.

It's a far-fetched scenario, the stuff of science fiction (and very similar to the main plot of the *Matrix* trilogy of films), but it's difficult to find a reason why it couldn't be possible. If you were a brain in a vat, how would you know that you were? And, more to the point, how do you know that you aren't a brain in a vat? Perhaps reality, or what you think is reality, is in fact a computer simulation – and one that you're not voluntarily choosing to participate in.

Dreams and illusions

You don't have to go into the realms of science fiction or fantasy to get an idea of how elusive the concept of reality is,

though. Long before computers or even most machines were invented, **Zhuangzi**, or Zhuang Zhou (*c.*369–286 BCE), realized that our minds can be fooled into thinking something is real, and that made him sceptical about the whole notion of reality. He'd ask you to think about what you experience when you're asleep, your dreams. You must have had dreams which, at the time, seemed so real. How do you know they weren't? And before you rush to answer that you realized it was only a dreamed once you woke up, he'd tell you a story of one of his dreams, when he dreamt he was a butterfly. In the dream, he lived happily as a butterfly, and didn't know that he was Zhuangzi. When he woke up, he realized that he was Zhuangzi. But he couldn't tell whether he was a man who had dreamed he was a butterfly, or a butterfly dreaming he was Zhuangzi. So don't be too harsh on your boyfriend's grasp on reality; you can't be too sure of your own.

That would be to excuse your boyfriend's antisocial behaviour, though, and let him off the hook by conceding that reality is a bit of a difficult concept to pin down. If you're looking for an explanation that will bring him to his senses, you could do worse than ask what **Plato** has to say on the subject. As it happens, he'd be quite happy to go along with the idea that what we think is reality

"To them, I said, the truth would be literally nothing but the shadows of the images"
Plato

Plato's cave

is in fact an illusion, but not some kind of computer-generated simulation, or even a dream. No, he'd say that there's more to reality than what we experience with our senses.

To explain what he means, Plato would tell you his "Allegory of the Cave", one of the best-known thought experiments of all time. It's the story of a group of people who have been held prisoner in a dark cave all their lives. They are made to sit facing the back of the cave, tied up so that they cannot turn their heads and all they can see is the back wall. Behind them, although they don't

know it, is a low wall, and beyond that a fire that dimly lights up the cave. From time to time, the people holding them captive walk around behind this wall, carrying all sorts of different objects, which cast shadows onto the back of the cave in front of the prisoners. These shadows are the only things that the prisoners have ever seen, and they have no idea that anything else exists. So, they have nothing else to form an idea of reality from, other than those shadows.

Now, if you untie one of the prisoners and let her get up and turn around, she'll quite literally see the light, and it will take

> *"I do not believe that I am now dreaming, but I cannot prove that I am not. I am, however, quite certain that I am having certain experiences, whether they be those of a dream or those of waking life"*
> Bertrand Russell

a moment for her eyes to adjust to it. Then she'll realize, when she sees the objects and the fire, that what she had taken for reality were only shadows of what actually exists. Plato would argue that the prisoner's original perception of reality is like the one we have of the world through our senses: it's an illusory imitation of the real thing. Just like your boyfriend's world of virtual reality and online friends.

Rather than leave you feeling superior to you boyfriend, however, Plato would take the allegory a step further, showing you that your concept of reality is not that much better. The freed prisoner, having seen the error of mistaking the shadows for reality, gradually becomes accustomed to the light and notices the entrance to the cave. Making her way out into the open, she is confronted with the world outside, and the bright light of the sun. And, naturally, she will be dazzled by everything that she sees, the world as it really is.

Like the prisoner, you have not only got to recognize that what you experience in this world is a shadow, an illusion, but also to discover the ultimate reality, the world of things as they really are, which lies outside your experience.

But Plato would also mention that there is a snag when it comes to trying to wean your boyfriend off his computer habit. Once the prisoner had seen what there was outside the cave, she rushed back in to tell the others what she had discovered. And, of course, they didn't believe her. Telling your boyfriend his ersatz reality is just that is likely to get a similarly incredulous reaction.

Making a decision

If you want to forgive your BF's antisocial habit, Epicurus and Bentham would provide ample justification for his seeking pleasure and avoiding harsh reality. If you need a counterargument, however, Nozick suggests rational people would prefer reality to escapism. But before pronouncing on your boyfriend's love of virtual reality, consider what Putnam, Zhuangzi and Plato have to say about your own grasp on reality.

My new lover seems to be obsessed with the physical side of our relationship, but I'm not that interested. Is there something wrong with me?

Marquis de Sade • Foucault • Mill • Zhuangzi • Protagoras • Dennett

Everything was going so well, too, wasn't it? You found that the two of you had so much in common, sharing the same interests and even enjoying the same kinds of food. Until it came to the bedroom. And that's when you discovered that your appetites didn't exactly coincide. You're taken aback that your new caring and considerate soulmate is a more enthusiastic lover than you had bargained for, and it's making you feel uncomfortable. Now you're beginning to question not just your relationship, but also whether you're undersexed or being prudish.

Let's start by, if you'll excuse the expression, getting things straight. Is your reaction to your lover's ardour simply because your physical needs are different, or is there an element of moral judgement in there too? That is to say, do you really have less interest in sex, or is it that you regard it as somehow sinful? Maybe you're not too happy with the concept of enjoying the pleasures of the flesh at all, and believe that sex should be a serious business. You wouldn't be alone in that, so you're not abnormal, and in that sense there's nothing wrong with you, other than being a bit prissy. But it could be argued that there's nothing wrong with enjoying your sex life either, and indulging in whatever gives you and your partner pleasure.

If you were to ask Donatien Alphonse François, **Marquis de Sade** (1740–1814),

he'd tell you that you're missing out on a lot of fun, just because you've been brought up to believe that it's a sin to have a good time. But his so-called philosophizing on the subject of freedom from conventional morality, religion and law was just a thinly veiled excuse for him to revel in his hedonistic pursuits. And then write about them in salacious detail. You'd do better to look to a much better philosopher such as **Michel Foucault** (1926–84), to argue the case against restrictive puritanical mores.

Far from just dismissing conventional sexual morality, Foucault would tell you that he recognizes why you might recoil from the idea of indulging in carnal pleasures. It's not that you are innately opposed to those sensual delights, but that you have been conditioned to find them distasteful

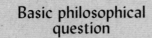

Basic philosophical question

Is it morally wrong to enjoy sensual pleasures? Do the conventions of our society dictate what we see as morally right and wrong? Do other people experience things the same way as I do?

by the society you live in. Family, religion, government and other institutions have all had an influence on your thinking, ensuring your notions of what is right and wrong, acceptable and unacceptable, conform to convention – and most of them give the message that it's wicked to seek sexual gratification. It's so deeply ingrained, you probably don't even know that your emotional reactions are being manipulated. Because of your upbringing, you react to deviations from this social norm with shame, fear or even revulsion.

The end result is that, because you are bound by convention, you are inhibited. If you can overcome your fear of breaking with convention, you can begin to enjoy things more than you dared to think. In fact, you

have to dare to think that you will enjoy them, in order to break away from the power of convention. In any case, we're talking about making love, a way of giving and receiving pleasure, so what can possibly be morally wrong with that? What harm does it do anybody?

John Stuart Mill (1806–73), a rather studious and correct Victorian English gentleman, and Foucault might seem strange bedfellows, but on this the two would agree. Mill would argue that if it doesn't hurt anybody, it's nobody else's business. He might add, however, that he would probably sympathize if you said that you preferred a good book to a roll in the hay, but that's up to you. Nobody can tell you what you should or shouldn't get up to in the privacy of your own bedroom, so long as it's between consenting adults. But consent is crucial: you're the only one who can decide what to do with your body – and what you let other people do with your body.

Showing your feelings

It's possible, though, that for whatever reason, you just don't enjoy erotic activities, in the same way that some people don't like football. One man's meat, as relativist philosophers might put it, is another man's poison. If you say that you don't enjoy football, fair enough. And if you

> "*Over his own body and mind, the individual is sovereign*"
> John Stuart Mill

> *"You young maidens, too long constrained by a fanciful Virtue's absurd and dangerous bonds and by those of a disgusting religion imitate the fiery Eugénie; be as quick as she to destroy, to spurn all those ridiculous precepts inculcated in you by imbecile parents"*
> Donatien Alphonse François, Marquis de Sade

say you don't like sex, nobody should be able to argue with that either. It's a matter of personal taste, and there can't be any definitive rules about things that are subjective – nobody can tell you what you do or don't enjoy.

Or can they? **Zhuangzi** would disagree. Although you can't tell people what they should or shouldn't like, he says that you can tell whether they actually do enjoy something or not. He makes his point with the story of when he was watching fish playing in a river, and remarked how much they were enjoying themselves. His friend Huizi asked how he knew they were enjoying themselves, when Zhuangzi himself was not a fish, to which Zhuangzi replied that Huizi was not Zhuangzi, so how could he be sure that Zhuangzi didn't know the fish were enjoying themselves. Huizi was forced to admit he didn't know what Zhuangzi did or didn't know, because he wasn't Zhuangzi. Anyway, continued Zhuangzi, by asking the question "How do you know?" Huizi was implicitly admitting that Zhuangzi did know that the fish were having a good time, and was just asking how he got that knowledge. Zhuangzi's clincher was to say that he knew they were enjoying themselves, because he could see them having a good time.

Which is a somewhat complicated way of saying that you don't have to be someone else to know what they're feeling. You can tell what people like or dislike by their behaviour, by their responses to different stimuli. If you give a child a piece of chocolate, you'll get a smile; if you prick her with a pin, she'll cry out in pain. You don't have to actually be that child to know what she likes and dislikes, because you can tell by the way she reacts to things.

Protagoras would point out a flaw in that line of reasoning, though. A person's reactions, whether they are a cry of pain or a shout of joy, only tell us so much. He would probably argue that it's what a person is actually feeling or thinking that matters, not what outward signs they're showing. We each experience things in our own way – you like the taste of garlic, but other people

Zhuangzi was sure he knew when fish were having fun. But perhaps what he saw as play was not a game, but an instinctive reaction or a struggle for survival?

39

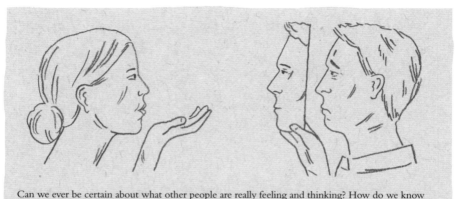

Can we ever be certain about what other people are really feeling and thinking? How do we know they're not hiding their true feelings, or even that they have any feelings at all?

can't stand it. It could be that you actually experience the taste of garlic in entirely different ways, and that would explain your different preferences. Perhaps when you taste something sweet, your experience is what another person would recognize as bitter. There's no way of knowing.

Nor can we be sure that what you experience as pain isn't the sensation your partner would identify as pleasure. Zhuangzi would interrupt at this point, to say that the responses to pain and pleasure are involuntary, and universally recognized, so good evidence of whether that person likes or dislikes the experience, even if we don't know exactly what sensation she's feeling. Just so, Protagoras replies, but reactions could be just as subjective as the sensations they are responding to. If someone cries out "Ow" when pricked with a pin, this could be their involuntary reaction to what is to them a pleasurable sensation – or at least what you would describe as a pleasurable sensation.

Philosophical zombies
Take your situation. You could give in to all your lover's requests for long lovemaking sessions, and pretend to enjoy them. And your partner would not know that you're faking it. In fact, your partner couldn't interpret your responses with any certainty: are those moans of pleasure? Or discomfort? Or just boredom? But at the same time, you can't be sure of what your lover is experiencing.

> "To do as one would be done by, and to love one's neighbour as oneself, constitute the ideal perfection of utilitarian morality"
> John Stuart Mill

> *"Reason is, and ought only to be the slave of the passions, and can never pretend to any other office than to serve and obey them"*
>
> David Hume

Daniel Dennett (b. 1942) would go even further with this argument, saying that we can never know for certain what is going on in someone else's mind. More than that, response to a stimulus isn't even evidence that somebody is experiencing anything at all – they may just be going through the motions. After all, it wouldn't be difficult to make a machine that purred with pleasure when you stroked it, so it's not beyond the bounds of possibility to construct an android programmed to respond to stimuli just like a human. But of course, it wouldn't have any feelings or consciousness. So, it's possible, Dennett suggests, that there may be creatures who look just like human beings, who react just like humans to pain, pleasure and so on, but are no more than organic machines programmed to react in particular ways to certain stimuli.

Dennett called these creatures "zombies", but these philosophical zombies are rather different from the Haitian voodoo creatures and the undead flesh-eating monsters of horror movies. In every respect, they are indistinguishable from humans, except they have no consciousness or feelings. Not as dangerous as a Hollywood zombie, then, but just as chilling, as you have no way of telling whether someone is a zombie or not. Your new lover, for instance. Or anybody, for that matter. Perhaps everybody except you is a zombie...

No matter how much the idea flies in the face of common sense, it's difficult to find a rational argument to disprove the existence of philosophical zombies. Nevertheless, it's extremely unlikely that they exist, and more than likely that other people have feelings and consciousness just like you, judging by the fact their reactions are just like yours.

But, like orgasms, they could be faked.

Making a decision

Maybe you're doubting whether your attitudes to sex are "normal". It may be that de Sade and Foucault have a point about repressive sexual mores being imposed on us by society. It's possible, however, that as Protagoras says, you and your lover enjoy different things. But can either of you really know what the other enjoys, as Zhuangzi asserts, or is Dennett right to say that other people's minds are a closed book to us?

My partner bought me a pair of shoes for my birthday, but I think they're really ugly.

Plato • Aristotle • Protagoras • Kant

Now, you could just smile and say thank you, to avoid hurting your partner's feelings. Or you could try to show him how wrong he is about what looks good. Naturally, he thinks the shoes are beautiful, and to him that isn't just an opinion, it's a fact. But without disputing that's what he honestly feels, you're equally sure they're pretty hideous. You can't both be right. Or can you? What is beauty, anyway – is it something that can be objectively assessed, or just a matter of taste?

Beware: you're going to have a hard time convincing your partner. It's not just that you disagree about those damned shoes, but you probably have opposing views on the very nature of beauty, corresponding to the two main philosophical approaches to the question of beauty.

Ancient Greece is justly famous for its artistic achievements, which have influenced and inspired Western culture right up to the present, so it's no surprise to find that the notion of "beauty" was a hot topic among classical Greek philosophers. Like other abstract concepts such as "virtue" and "justice", it proved difficult to define, and inevitably there were differences of opinion on the subject.

On the one hand, **Plato** took an absolutist stance. Beauty, he said, is truth, and truth beauty. And just as something is either true or not, there aren't degrees of beauty, it is an absolute, an ideal. There is, he believed, such as thing as perfect beauty, a concept rather than a thing, which exists in a world of ideal "forms" that we can access with our minds and reason, rather than with our senses. We recognize beauty in the things that we experience with our senses because we can relate them to that ideal form of beauty.

As always, his protégé **Aristotle** took an opposing stance, dismissing the idea of an ideal form of beauty, and instead suggesting that we may not be able to define beauty, but can recognize individual instances of it when we come across them. And from the many and various things that we encounter that we

> *"Beauty is in the eye of the beholder"*
> English proverb

Dress sense, and other matters of taste, can be influenced by culture.

call beautiful, we can build up a composite idea of the elements that constitute beauty – in the case of the classical Greeks these were things such as balance, harmony, symmetry and mathematical ratios.

But while Plato and Aristotle disagreed about how we arrive at our notions of beauty, they both believed that something that is beautiful has attributes that make it so or, in other words, that beauty is something that is inherent in an object. And if that is the case, then there must be ways of telling whether something has or doesn't have that quality, some sort of objective criteria for judging beauty.

An inherent quality?

Needless to say, there were philosophers who disputed this. On the other side of the divide were those taking a relativist viewpoint, foremost among them orator and lawyer **Protagoras**. He pointed out that ideas of what is beautiful in a person, such as body

shape or skin colour, differed from place to place and even time to time, so beauty cannot be absolute and universal, but may be culturally determined. What's more, if beauty is relative, there is no objective means of saying what is or isn't beautiful, so any judgement of beauty is subjective. And if beauty is indeed in the eye of the beholder, then it isn't an inherent quality of an object, but something that the viewer brings to it.

The subjectivist would also argue that if beauty is an inherent property of something, it would still be beautiful even if there were no humans to appreciate it. That's a pretty difficult case to answer, so perhaps the whole notion of beauty is a human construct; it is human judgement that makes something beautiful, it is a subjective thing. And yet, we instinctively feel that it can't be merely subjective, that there are some things that can be universally recognized as attractive or repulsive – and these may have a biological function, such as sexual attraction or a sense

> "When [a man] puts a thing on a pedestal and calls
> it beautiful, he demands the same delight from others."
> Immanuel Kant

of repulsion at the sight of maggots, and are "hard-wired" into us.

So, let's leave the last word with **Immanuel Kant**, who neatly brought the two sides a bit closer together with his suggestion of "universal validity". Our notions of beauty are, he conceded, based on a subjective response, but are so much a part of our culture that they can be considered universally valid. There is a general consensus about the things that are considered beautiful, and those that are considered repulsive. There is, of course, a fair amount of wiggle room between those two extremes, which would explain the difference of opinion between you and your partner. It may not convince you that your shoes are beautiful, but maybe it will stop you falling out over the issue.

Making a decision

Do you think, like Plato and Aristotle, that there are objective criteria that define what is beautiful, and that the shoes don't measure up to these? According to Plato and Aristotle, beauty is an inherent quality, but you might prefer to think, like Protagoras, that our ideas of beauty are subjective, that beauty is in the eye of the beholder, and that our assessment of beauty isinfluenced by cultural norms.

Basic philosophical question

Is beauty inherent in a thing, or is it something that we bring to a thing?

"The chief forms of beauty are order and symmetry and definiteness, which the mathematical sciences demonstrate in a special degree"

Aristotle

Work

Chapter 2

Is it OK to hurt others on my way to a big promotion?

Confucius • Mill • Kant • Machiavelli • Bentham • Nietzsche

So, you're not content to stay in the job you've got, and feel that you are capable of much more. There's a chance of a big promotion, and you believe you're the person for the job. It's not just about personal ambition or even the money: you've got a lot to offer, and it will be good for you and good for the firm. But it's a dog-eat-dog world out there, and to get the job, you'll have to be quite ruthless. Can you justify maybe ruining your colleagues' careers on your way to the top?

The nub of the problem here is that, although you think that it is right for you to get the promotion, at the same time you instinctively feel it is wrong to harm other people. This feeling, that harming people is morally wrong, is deeply ingrained in all of us, and lies at the heart of moral philosophy. It comes from our ability to put ourselves in other people's shoes, to recognize that they can be hurt in the same way as ourselves. And this notion of reciprocity gives rise to a maxim that is often referred to as the *golden rule*: do as you would be done by.

So, if you're looking for moral guidance in going for that promotion, here's a rule that puts it in a nutshell. And it's one that has been adopted by almost every religion around the world, in one form or another, as well as a good few moral philosophers.

Even **Confucius** (551–479 BCE), whose philosophy was less about theoretical religious rights and wrongs than the practical business of running an imperial court, gave the rule as "do not do to others what you wouldn't want them to do to you".

Much later, **John Stuart Mill** passionately argued for the liberty of the individual to do whatever he or she wanted in pursuit of happiness, but incorporated the principle of the golden rule, by adding the proviso so long as it doesn't harm others or interfere with them doing what they want.

Rules, or guidelines?

Probably the philosopher most associated with laying down the law when it came to morality was **Immanuel Kant**. For him, if something is morally wrong, there's no

> "*A man who strives after goodness in all his acts is sure to come to ruin, since there are so many men who are not good*"
> Niccolò Machiavelli

> *"Always recognize that human individuals are ends, and do not use them as means to your end"*
> Karl Popper paraphrasing Immanuel Kant

ducking the issue, it's always wrong. This is, he said, a categorical imperative. And fundamental to his moral philosophy was the idea that individual people, all of us, should be treated as ends, never as means to an end. Which is a highfaluting way of saying that you should never use other people to get what you want, and in this case it is just plain wrong to treat them as stepping stones on your climb to the top.

But perhaps it's not quite as clear-cut as that. It's all very well having moral "laws" that we can use to guide our actions, but life isn't always that simple. Maybe we should consider the bigger picture, too, and judge the morality of something by the end result. **Niccolò Machiavelli** (1469–1527) would agree. He created quite a stir with his little handbook for rulers, *The Prince*, in which he suggested that the sort of moral laws put forward by the Church needn't always apply.

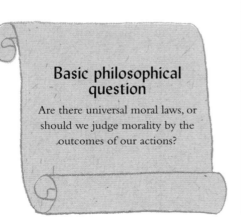

Basic philosophical question

Are there universal moral laws, or should we judge morality by the outcomes of our actions?

A lot of the time, Machiavelli said, we have to bend or even break the rules in order to get things done, and this can be justified if it is for the greater good. There may be some collateral damage, but in the end things work out for the best.

Harm and happiness

Although they might not be as ruthless as Machiavelli, a number of philosophers took his point, that rather than attempting to find and live by unbreakable moral rules, we should think about the outcomes of our actions. Utilitarianism, an idea pioneered by **Jeremy Bentham**, was based on this new way of looking at morality. In brief, he proposed that the moral worth of an

> *"The bite of conscience: a sign that the character*
> *is no match for the deed"*
> Friedrich Nietzsche

To achieve success, you sometimes have to be ruthless.

happiness (or least harm) for the greatest number.

If you feel that weighing up the morality of going for that promotion is problematic, you might prefer the advice of **Friedrich Nietzsche**, who rejected all that religious and moral hand-wringing as outdated and irrelevant. What interested him was the will of individuals to live life to the full, and achieve their potential. To do this, they would have to have what he called the "will to power", overcoming all obstacles, including other people, and especially their own conscience. So, if you haven't got the will to take the morally dubious actions to go for that promotion, and the pricks of conscience are holding you back, perhaps you're not really up to the job. Survival of the fittest...

action consisted of the amount of happiness it produced, and that the morally right thing to do was that which created the greatest

Making a decision

Confucius, Mill and most major religions tell us to "do as you would be done by", and you should ask yourself how you would feel if the situation were reversed. Kant would go further and say that if it's wrong to hurt someone, it's always wrong. But Machiavelli and Bentham advise you to look to the outcomes, what's best for everybody in the end, while Nietzsche would urge you to ignore your conscience in order to achieve your potential.

I'm nearly 50, FFS! I'm fed up with being an accountant – should I follow my dream of being a rock star?

Lao Tzu • Schopenhauer • Marx • Sartre

There comes a time for almost all of us when we take stock of our lives and, as often as not, find that they're lacking. When you look back on your life, you see your striving for security and stability as a waste of effort, and notice more clearly all the missed opportunities and frustrated dreams. You're showing the classic signs of a mid-life crisis, that realization that it's almost too late to do the things you missed out on. If you don't act on your impulses now, you never will. It's time to examine your options.

There's a note of urgency in the way you've framed your question. It's as if you've just realized that time's running out, and there are still things you want or even need to do, before it's too late. You've spent your life working at a job that gives you little satisfaction, to provide for a family that occupies most of the rest of your time, and you've had to put your dreams on the back burner. The frustration has finally caught up with you now, though, and your desire to catch up with those things is overwhelming, making what you've done thus far seem pointless in comparison.

That's the nub of the problem, **Lao Tzu**, also called Laozi (6th century BCE), would tell you – it's your desire that is causing you heartache. Not the disappointment of not having done something, but the desire to do something. Especially the sorts of desire that you have at your time of life. Let's face it, you're probably never going to make it in the music business at your age, are you? Yes, there

are lots of ageing superstars out there, but they started early, and are just resting on their laurels now.

The sad truth is that you're being unrealistic. Your dream of recording a great album and then taking your band on a world tour just isn't going to happen. Worse, if you fool yourself into believing that it's possible, you're only going to end up disappointed, even more disappointed than you are now.

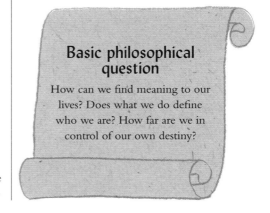

Basic philosophical question

How can we find meaning to our lives? Does what we do define who we are? How far are we in control of our own destiny?

Life is a constant process of dying

Schopenhauer

But if you don't at least have a shot at it, you're going to feel frustrated, and regret it for the rest of your life. Why put yourself through all of that, Lao Tzu would ask; wouldn't it be better to recognize that some things are out of your reach, and just let them go? Learn to be satisfied with what you've got, strive for the things that you can achieve and stop crying for the moon. Then you'll discover that you can find true happiness.

Not according to **Arthur Schopenhauer**, you can't. In contrast to what he would regard as Lao Tzu naive optimism, Schopenhauer argued that we can never achieve any real satisfaction. Life is a continual series of disappointments and frustrations, and the mid-life crisis is just a time when you become more aware of that fact. Take your situation now. If you do nothing, you're condemned to a miserable existence as an accountant, and probably an

unfulfilling home life as a result. Go ahead with your dream of becoming a rock star, he says, see where it gets you. It's more than likely that you'll fail dismally, like most aspiring musicians. All those hopes and dreams dashed. But let's just suppose your talent is recognized, and you get the stardom you've always hoped for. You'll most likely soon get fed up with the tedium of recording sessions, the grind of touring and the nuisance of paparazzi and undiscerning fans. And then start dreaming of a different kind of life.

Be honest, Schopenhauer tells you, it's the human condition to think that the grass is always greener on the other side, and then discover it's pretty tasteless wherever you look. It's not just that if you fail you'll be disappointed, but that, even if you succeed, it won't give you the satisfaction you thought it would. If you have a goal and achieve it, there's nothing left to strive for, and your life will seem empty. But if you don't try, you'll be continually wanting something you can't have. You just can't win. Life's like that – you can never satisfy your desires, so are doomed to a life of suffering.

And if you're thinking that getting yourself a fast little two-seater car, or exchanging your suit for that sexy casual look, or having a fling with someone 20 years your junior is going to help you magically regain your youth, take a look in the mirror. The only glimmer

"Without music, life would be a mistake"
Friedrich Nietzsche

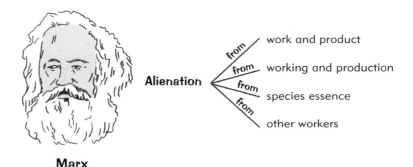

Marx

Alienation

- from work and product
- from working and production
- from species essence
- from other workers

of hope that Schopenhauer can offer is that one of your options is to do something creative. And for him, the only escape from the inevitable suffering life heaps upon us is in the arts, and especially that most abstract of arts, music. Although taking up the guitar won't make your life any less of a mess, at least it will give you some solace.

Get a life

Thank goodness, not all philosophers are as downright despondent as Schopenhauer. But many of them recognize how much being stuck in an unsatisfying job can affect your life. It was something **Karl Marx** (1818–83) was particularly concerned about, and he'd understand your desire to break away from the stultifying boredom of accountancy. Most people, he says, don't have the luxury of doing a job that they enjoy, that they can take a pride in and that gives them satisfaction. In the modern world, since industrialization, capitalists control the agenda as far as work is concerned, and unless you're one of the capitalist class, you're just a cog in the machinery of industry. As an accountant,

you know that all the bosses are concerned with is the bottom line, and the nature of work is determined by what is most productive and profitable, not what satisfies the workforce. And because they are reliant on capitalist industry to earn their meagre living, the workers are forced to do repetitive, demeaning, alienating and dangerous jobs that they can't afford to walk away from.

There are alternatives, however. At least, that's what existentialists would have you believe. **Jean-Paul Sartre** (1905–80), for example, would say that there is a point where you have to make a choice. That

We are our choices

Sartre

> *"The effect of music is so very much more powerful and penetrating than is that of the other arts, for these others speak only of the shadow, but music of the essence"*
> Arthur Schopenhauer

choice is generally precipitated by an existential crisis, such as the mid-life crisis you're experiencing, or the sort of angst you went through as a teenager, when you come face to face with the reality of your own mortality, and the fact that you really do exist, you have a life. And, in your case, that there's only so much of it left.

That's a tricky thing to make sense of, and most of us wonder if we can find any meaning to our lives. Sartre would say that that's up to you. Perhaps you find meaning in the work you do, but it's more likely that you realize there's more to life than simply going in to the office and trying to interpret balance sheets. Besides, he'd ask you, is that what you have chosen to do, or is it what has been expected of you, what other people have made you into?

There is no meaning to life, he says, except the meaning you give it. You can be defined by other people and their expectations, or you can define yourself. If you choose to be a rock guitarist, that's who you will be, much more than you consider yourself to be an accountant, because accountancy was the accepted career path for a person of your class and education. Just making a living is not going to give your life meaning, especially if it is no more than drudgery, but doing things, creating things and following your dreams will. So, dare to take a step into the unknown, live dangerously. Give yourself challenges, stretch yourself and experience the thrill of taking risks. If you don't make that choice now, you're forever going to be defined by someone else's agenda.

Making a decision

If you're yearning to do the things that you've always wanted to do before it's too late, you might want to consider what Lao Tzu has to say about the misery of desiring the unobtainable, and Schopenhauer's assertion that you can never achieve satisfaction, whatever you do. If that seems defeatist, you could take Marx's advice and break free from the shackles of capitalism, or Sartre's encouragement to find some meaning to your life.

Should I incriminate my colleague to avoid getting fired?

Nietzsche • Machiavelli • Hobbes • Rousseau • Smith • Nash

So, you and your workmate have been caught out, then. Just a minor infringement of company rules, but enough to get you into hot water. Your boss suspects (rightly, as it happens) that the two of you have been up to some much more serious stuff, but has no proof. Which is just as well, as that would get you both fired. He's prepared to cut a deal with you, though: incriminate your colleague for the big stuff, and you just get a slap on the wrist. If you don't, he'll come down on you hard.

This is a familiar situation, especially if you're a fan of gangster movies. The cops have caught a bad guy, but negotiate with his lawyer to drop the charges if he names names and testifies in court. The dilemma is between coming clean, doing the right thing by the law, or loyalty to comrades; playing by the rules, or honour among thieves. And on a purely practical level, weighing up whether police protection is sufficient to prevent any reprisals.

Some philosophers would tell you that to find an answer to this kind of problem, you should stop sweating about what's ethical, and concentrate on coming out of it to your best advantage. **Friedrich Nietzsche**, for example, would tell you to forget all that altruistic nonsense about loyalty and doing as you would be done by. That, in his opinion, is "slave morality", the code of ethics imposed on us by the religious establishment to stop us from getting ahead. You've got to overcome your qualms and misplaced ideas of morality in order to succeed. And don't think you will find it difficult to break with ideas of what's good and bad that have been drummed into you

since birth – you've already compromised your morality by committing the crime in the first place. Having taken that step into the world beyond good and evil, there's no turning back. Your loyalty is to yourself, not your colleague, or even your boss and the company. Take the best deal on offer. Turn the other guy in and get on with your life.

As you would expect, that's very much the advice **Niccolò Machiavelli** would give, too. Morals are all very well in your personal life, but this is business, and it's either kill or be killed. Your workmate knew just as well as

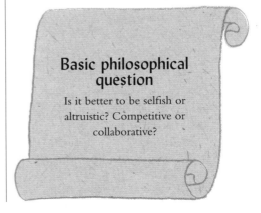

Basic philosophical question

Is it better to be selfish or altruistic? Competitive or collaborative?

> *"The RIGHT OF NATURE, which Writers commonly call Jus Naturale, is the Liberty each man hath, to use his own power, as he will himself, for the preservation of his own Nature; that is to say, of his own Life; and consequently, of doing any thing, which in his own Judgement, and Reason, he shall conceive to be the aptest means thereunto"*
> Thomas Hobbes

you what the stakes were when you decided to take the company for a ride, so he can't complain if he gets what's coming to him. All the same, nobody likes a snitch, so he might take it badly. If you are going to implicate him, make sure your boss gets him safely put away. But if there's any chance your partner in crime could get back at you, you might do better to take the rap for him. A sacrifice for you, but not just out of the kindness of your heart. Insurance, let's say. And you'll have him in your debt, too.

Self-interest

Not all philosophers are as ruthless as Machiavelli, however, and most would see your dilemma as a moral problem. But **Thomas Hobbes** (1588–1679) would be just as cynical about your motives. He would recognize that, although you might pretend you're trying to establish what would be the morally right thing to do, you're actually looking for what is right for you. It is, unfortunately, human nature to look after number one. That, he'd sternly tell you, is why we have rules and laws – to stop everyone from simply taking what they can, regardless of others. And in this case, your

boss is the authority, so you should do what he's asking you to do.

Nonsense, **Jean-Jacques Rousseau** (1712–78) would reply. What a jaundiced view of human nature. If it weren't for all the rules and regulations, this situation wouldn't have arisen. The system's at fault, according to Rousseau, because it doesn't appreciate things like friendship, loyalty and altruism, but instead values material things, and sets up laws to protect property. And that forces us into behaving in ways that go against our natural inclinations to co-operation and sharing. You've been put into a dog-eat-dog situation by your boss, who is manipulating the situation to his own advantage. What's more, it was probably because of his selfishness, greed and possessiveness of his property that you took advantage of the company to start with. Don't do any deals with him, Rousseau would tell you; go and talk to your colleague about it. Humans are by nature collaborative creatures, not motivated simply by what they can get for themselves. Both you and your boss have been corrupted by the rules of the establishment, but there is something you can do to change that: talk to your co-workers and come to a collective decision about how

Philosopher	Action
Machiavelli	Ignore morality, act in self-interest
Rousseau	Question the rules and collaborate with the accused
Smith	Ignore morality, act rationally
Hobbes	Obey the rules

this situation can be resolved, and how to stop it from being repeated.

Two conflicting ideas of human nature there, then. What you do depends, it would seem, on which of them you identify with. But **Adam Smith** (1723–90) has a more moderate opinion of human nature, covering the middle ground between those two extremes. As an economist, he concentrates not so much on what people should and shouldn't do, but on what they actually do, the way they behave. And he comes to the conclusion that we generally act in our own self-interest, but that doesn't mean we can't be altruistic too. It's how a market economy works, he'd explain. People don't produce goods and services out of the goodness of their hearts, but because they want to make money for themselves. Obviously, they have to take into account what other people

want, and are pleased when their goods are appreciated, but that's not their primary motivation.

Because we all behave in that way, making things and doing things in order to put money in our own pockets, but at the same time providing things that other people need and want, we all get something out of it. It's not just self-interest, however. Smith would argue that although our instincts are to look after ourselves first, we're also rational creatures, and if we examine our behaviour, it make sense to act in this way.

In answer to your problem then, he'd ask you to examine the dilemma rationally, not on the basis of morality, but what is in your best interests. Then see if that might also have the effect of providing something that is in someone else's interests too. Let's consider your options. You could come clean with

"*It is not from the benevolence of the butcher, the brewer or the baker that we expect our dinner, but from their regard to their own interest*"
Adam Smith

your boss and incriminate your colleague: that would be best for you, and would incidentally be of use to your boss, but would be harmful to your workmate. Or you could protect your friend, but then both you and your boss would lose out on the deal.

Put like that, it looks like you and your workmate are pitted against each other. Competition, Smith would tell you, is generally a good thing for the consumer, as it helps to encourage productivity and keep prices down. But it isn't necessarily so good for the producers. We're sort of programmed to think of competition as healthy for business, but Smith would point out that, in at least some cases, the rational thing to do, the thing that would be in our own best interests, would be to collaborate, not compete. In business, producers make bargains, and pool their resources to take advantage of economies of scale and a more efficient labour force. More cynically they can also form cartels, virtual monopolies, so that their customers have no choice but to buy their products at the prices they set. Smith would therefore advise you to see what benefit you get from making a deal with your boss, but also see if you can do a deal with your mate that is better.

Win or lose

It takes a mathematician to tell us the really rational thing to do: **John Forbes Nash** (1928–2015), a pioneer of *game theory*, which has made many philosophers take a fresh look at questions of morality. If we look at situations in life as kinds of game, Nash says, then we're making an assumption that success is all about winning – that games are competitive. If we change our mindset, however, we can see that many situations are not about one side winning and the other

	A keeps quiet	A incriminates B
B keeps quiet	Both A and B get disciplined. (win – win) ✔✔	B gets fired and goes to jail. A goes free. (lose big – win big) ✘✔
B incriminates A	B goes free. A gets fired and goes to jail. (win big – lose big) ✔✘	Both A and B get fired. (lose – lose) ✘✘

> "A less obvious type of application (of non-cooperative games) is to the study of cooperative games. By a cooperative game we mean a situation involving a set of players, pure strategies, and payoffs as usual; but with the assumption that the players can and will collaborate"
> John Forbes Nash

losing, but that there can be an outcome where both sides benefit. But this means abandoning the idea of competition, and taking on board an element of cooperation. If you take your situation, you could look at it as a competition between you and your colleague: you win, he loses, or vice versa.

But there is an alternative. Let's say you and your workmate have been caught driving company vehicles for personal use. The boss knows that you have also been stealing company property, but can't prove it. He offers you a deal: confess and incriminate your workmate, and you get off scot free, while he gets fired and prosecuted; or, if you stay silent, you'll face disciplinary action and a pay cut. You know he's offering your colleague the same deal. If you both confess and incriminate each other, you'll both get fired, but the boss wouldn't press criminal charges.

What should you do? Obviously, you stand to win big (or at least, lose nothing) if you confess, but the risk is that he'll do the same – and you stand to lose your job if he does. If you stay silent, you could end up without a job and in jail if he turns you in, but just get a slap on the wrist and a pay cut if he keeps quiet too. So the best thing for you both is to cooperate and both keep your mouths shut. It's a win–win situation. If you don't collaborate, the stakes are that much higher. And it's a solution that probably sits best with your conscience too.

Making a decision

If this is simply a matter of self-preservation, you could turn to Nietzsche and Machiavelli for support of your actions. You may think that's reverting to the law of the jungle, though, and look to Hobbes or Rousseau for a political ruling. Alternatively, you could seek a more rational answer, such as the ones from Smith or Nash, which would be in everybody's best interests.

I'll swear my computer has a mind of its own...

Turing • Searle • Descartes • Ryle

Most of the time, your computer does exactly what you tell it to do. And then, some days, it won't respond at all, or just goes its own sweet way. It's almost as if it's refusing to do what you're asking it. That's ridiculous, of course, because it's only a machine, an inanimate object, but it sometimes behaves as if it really has got a mind of its own. You're letting your imagination run away with itself, reading things into what your computer is doing, because machines can't think. Or at least, they don't think like we do.

And while most of your colleagues would agree, and laugh at the idea your computer is being wilfully disobedient, they might admit to a small but nagging doubt. Perhaps the machine on your desk today isn't capable of thinking in the same way as humans do, but might it be possible to make a computer that can? Although it sounds like the stuff of science fiction, it's not inconceivable.

In the early days of computer science, the subject of artificial intelligence was a hot topic, and pioneers in the field such as **Alan Turing** (1912–54) were tempted to indulge

in some philosophical speculation. As soon as it became clear that it would be possible to build a programmable calculating machine, an early precursor to what we today would call a computer, people asked, "Can machines think?" Turing realized that they wouldn't be satisfied by a simple yes or no answer, and suggested that there could be some kind of scientific test to determine whether a machine is showing signs of intelligence.

Put to the test

Turing's test was a simple one, based on a parlour game popular at the time. In this "imitation game", two players, a man and a woman, are put into a separate room, and a third player asks them questions that they answer in writing. The interrogator then has to try to decide which of the two interviewees is the woman, and which the man. In the "Turing test", the rules are the same, but instead of a man and a woman, the questions are answered by a human and a machine. Turing would emphasize that this wasn't a test of ability to give correct answers (which an advanced computer would be able to do more accurately than a human), but answers that a human would give.

The machine is considered to have passed the test if the questioner cannot tell by their answers which is the computer and which the human. However, and this is where Turing would stray from the scientific to the philosophical, what does it mean for the machine to have passed the test? He would say that a machine that gives answers indistinguishable from a human's answers is showing intelligence. Artificial intelligence, but intelligence nonetheless. And when pressed to answer the question, "Is it thinking?", he'd smile and tell you that it isn't thinking in the same way as we think of thinking, but what else would you call what it's doing? It depends, he thinks, on what you mean by "think".

You might feel that Turing's dodging the issue a bit. You don't doubt that your

Basic philosophical question

Can machines think? Are they capable of understanding or consciousness? Are our brains like computers? Or do we have minds that are separate from our bodies?

computer is doing something, and that that appears to be thinking, but you want to know if it has a mind of its own, whether it has some idea of what it's doing, some intention of doing it. **John Searle** (b. 1932) would try to convince you that your first instincts are correct: computers don't really know what they're doing. To prove his point, he'd tell you that he has a program that can process questions written in Mandarin, in Chinese characters, and give intelligible and correct answers, also in Chinese. It does it so well that a computer using this program would pass the Turing test, being indistinguishable from a human to a Chinese speaker. Now, says Searle, imagine a person who has no knowledge of Chinese is put into a room where she has access to all the information in that computer program. She is then given written questions in Chinese. She can follow the instructions of the program, and produce a convincing reply in Chinese. Without understanding a single Chinese character.

Isn't that, Searle would ask, exactly what the computer is doing? Following instructions, without any understanding of what it's doing, but giving the impression it knows what it's doing? He argues that thinking, surely, involves understanding what you're thinking about. What machines lack is consciousness, that combination of understanding, feeling, sense, awareness and intention, among other things. So you can't describe what your computer is doing as "thinking", and if it isn't thinking, it can't be

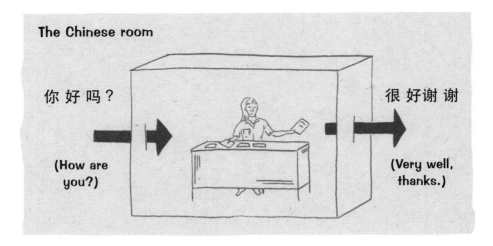

The Chinese room

你 好 吗 ？

(How are you?)

很 好 谢 谢

(Very well, thanks.)

said to have a mind at all.

Let's turn the argument on its head for a moment, though. If machines can't think, because they haven't got a mind, what about us humans? Isn't our brain just a sophisticated organic computer? Not according to **René Descartes** (1596–1650), who would argue that humans are unique in having both a physical body and a non-physical mind. He reached that conclusion, he would explain, by a scientific process: if he had no rational grounds to believe something was incontrovertibly true, he discounted it.

Imagine, he would say, that there is an evil demon determined to torment you. This little devil has the ability to make you doubt everything you know about the world about you. He has the ability to deceive every one of your physical senses, so you can't believe what you're seeing, hearing, feeling or anything else. And if you can't believe anything your body is telling you, it may be that it doesn't exist at all, and you have to doubt your very existence.

The ghost in the machine

Not so fast, though; let's not jump to conclusions. If you doubt your existence, there must be a thing that is doing the doubting, and that thing must be you. You're thinking, so you exist – or, as Descartes put it, "*Cogito ergo sum*" (I think therefore I am). But because you've already established that your physical being could be an illusion, this "you" must be something else, a non-physical thing capable of thinking, quite separate from your body. This, Descartes would tell you, is what some people would call the spirit or soul, but he recognizes as the mind.

If you then shake off the deceiving demon, and come back to your senses, so to speak, you'll realize that your body gives you information about the material world, while your mind processes the information of your mental world. Although your body and mind are two separate entities, and are of two different substances, material and immaterial, they are obviously linked and able to interact. The interface between them, he explains, is in the brain (specifically situated near the pineal gland).

Gilbert Ryle (1900–76), however, would tell you that Descartes was talking utter rubbish. Ryle thought that Descartes was guilty of confusing two different kinds of things: the physical body with its sense organs and brain, and their properties and functions. It's like the difference between the abstract concept of "the electorate", compared to the flesh-and-blood people who have the power to vote. They both exist, of course, but are in different categories, just as both mind and body exist. The fundamental error Descartes made was a category mistake, assuming that mind and body are the same type of thing, even if they are separate, and this led him to the entirely false conclusion that there is some kind of "ghost in the machine". There isn't. You have a mental life which is a property, a function of your physical body, and the two are different but inseparable. There's nothing more to us physically than the various materials our bodies are made of, and what we call our minds is a description of one of its properties.

And if there's no "ghost" in the machine of the human body, why should a machine be anything other than the materials it is made out of? There's certainly no "ghost" in your computer, and its "mind" is only what it does, what it is programmed to do. And, as yet, nobody has worked out what consciousness actually is, so it's not likely that anybody could program a computer to have any awareness, intention or understanding of what it's doing. On the other hand, our brains are just a collection of cells forming a network of electrical impulses, and yet they allow us to think and have consciousness – why should a collection of sophisticated electronic circuitry be any different? Couldn't what they are doing be described as thinking?

Making a decision

Can computers think? It depends what we mean by "thinking" – and Turing and Searle offer two different ways of looking at whether what computers do is really thinking, or just processing information. Is that any different from what our brains do, though? You might agree with Descartes that our minds are separate from our physical bodies, or with Ryle that there is no "ghost in the machine".

How come I've got to work overtime just to survive, while some people make a fortune for doing next to nothing?

Socrates • Aristotle • Paine • Rousseau • Cicero • Rawls • Nozick

Sometimes it seems as if there's no justice in the world. You do your best to live a decent life and provide for your family, but it's a constant struggle making ends meet. At the same time as you're putting in the extra hours, your boss is making his way to the golf course after a short meeting and a long lunch. And he takes home a hundred times what you do! What gives him the right to do that? It's just not fair...

Put like that, it does sound like you're getting a raw deal. And you're not the only one – there are people all over the world working hard for a pittance, while a few live in luxury. You'd think that after several thousand years of civilization, we would have created a fairer form of society, but if anything it seems the gap between rich and poor is getting wider. And that can't be right, can it?

Actually, it's a question that has occupied

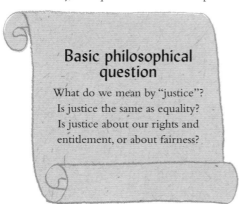

Basic philosophical question

What do we mean by "justice"?
Is justice the same as equality?
Is justice about our rights and entitlement, or about fairness?

philosophers since classical Greek times, when the Athenians set up a society that prided itself on its principles of democracy and justice. But there was a thorn in Athens's side: **Socrates**, who wasn't content to simply accept the way things were, but wanted to question the system (and everything else) to see if they were getting it right. If you told him your grievances, he wouldn't agree or disagree, nor offer any sympathy or advice. Instead, he'd start asking you what you thought, and what exactly you meant.

That's the trouble with turning to Socrates for advice. His answer to everything is "Yes, but...", followed by series of questions that get you doubting what you said in the first place. It's his way of getting to the nub of any problem, before attempting to come up with a solution. Although it can be irritating, he does get you to think about things such as justice, and what exactly you mean when you say something is unjust. In this case, he'd pick up on your idea that "it's not fair". What

do you mean, "fair"? Do you mean "equal" – that you and your boss have unequal workloads, and are getting unequal rewards? Or do you mean "just"? Do you think it's unjust that you work harder for less return than someone else? Are justice and equality the same thing, then? And if not, what do you think "justice" is?

Justice and equality

All you did was point out that it doesn't seem fair that some people are better off than others, and now Socrates is challenging you to define "justice". And that's no easy task, as most of the Greek philosophers will tell you. **Aristotle**, for example, would say that we can usually recognize when something is just or unjust, but can't say what justice itself is. Like many abstract concepts, we know it when we see it, but can't actually define it.

He would also try to explain the difference between justice and equality, that although equality is a form of justice, justice doesn't always mean the same thing as equality.

Which takes us to the problem of defining what we mean by "equality". Are there different kinds of equality? Just as the Athenians had aimed to create a just society, the thinkers behind the revolutions in America and France in the 18th century wanted to create a more equal society. Your complaint about working hard and earning little, while others do little and earn lots, was a major concern for **Thomas Paine** (1737–1809). He'd tell you that the injustice was due to privilege. Some people are born into positions of power and wealth, and others just don't get a look in. But that can be

"*The money that we possess is the instrument of liberty, that which we lack and strive to obtain is the instrument of slavery*"
Jean-Jacques Rousseau

remedied by giving everybody (well, all adult white men) the same rights to certain things, an equality of opportunity. He'd proudly explain that he set the ball rolling with his *Rights of Man*, leading to a call for the rights of women, and the civil rights movement in the 20th century, and the eventual Universal Declaration of Human Rights. Equal rights for all – now there's justice for you!

Hold on, **Jean-Jacques Rousseau** would say. It's all very well having equality of opportunity in law, but that's not much consolation if the system still denies you the ability to do anything about it. Besides, he would point out, all that talk of "rights" is part of the problem. It's not just privilege that leads to injustice, it's entitlement – our society is geared to protecting some people's rights, especially rights of ownership, while only giving lip service to others. The law, which should be ensuring justice, is all about protecting property, and favours the haves over the have-nots. The root cause of the problem, according to Rousseau, is property, and there is an unequal distribution of wealth. No matter what your rights are, there will be no equality of outcome until that's tackled. Do away with the idea of private property ownership, and give everyone an equal stake in the wealth of the community.

Fairness and entitlement

Two different kinds of equality, then – of opportunity, and of outcome. Paine's equal rights, or Rousseau's equal share. Both seem to have some claim to being a form of justice,

and satisfy **Cicero's** (106–43 BCE) idea that "Justice renders to every one his due". The problem is, how do you decide who is due what? Two American philosophers, **John Rawls** (1921–2002) and **Robert Nozick**, came up with very different answers to that, in explanations of the concept of justice that echo the Rousseau–Paine arguments.

Rawls would look at your situation and agree with you that it isn't fair. And fairness, for him, is the principle underlying justice. But, he'd ask, would you be crying, "It's not fair!" if you happened to be born into privilege and went straight to the top of an industry earning a fortune? You might privately admit that it isn't exactly just, but you wouldn't complain. No, the high earners dismiss calls for equality from the workers as the "politics of envy", while the low earners denounce rising inequality as the "politics of greed". They can't both be right, but is there a way of coming up with a fairer arrangement? Rawls thinks there is. Imagine, he says, you were starting a business with others, and didn't know whether you were going to be the boss, middle management or one of the workers on the shop floor: how would this affect the way you decided the pay structure and length of the working day? Because you're working from behind what he calls a "veil of ignorance" about your place in that firm, you will almost certainly opt for an equitable system that is fair for everybody.

Nozick, however, doesn't see it that way at all. He identifies the principle of justice as entitlement – not privilege, but

> ## "Whatever arises from a just situation by just steps is itself just"
> Robert Nozick

"The principles of justice are chosen behind a veil of ignorance"
John Rawls

legal entitlement – and that may result in inequality that you find unfair, but is nevertheless just. If you own something, nobody else is entitled to it unless you sell or give it to them, or you have acquired it from them illegitimately (by stealing or cheating, for example). So, from a starting point where everybody has the property they're entitled to, whether that's goods, land or money, they can engage in a process of free exchange with others, with their consent. So long as the transactions are legitimate, everyone will be entitled to what they own, so the distribution that results from this process will be just, even if there are large inequalities. So, rectifying the unfairness of your situation by reducing your boss's wealth and increasing yours would be unjust – and that includes taking money from him in taxes to redistribute wealth. Whether you like it or not, he's perfectly entitled as manager or owner of the firm to what he's got, so long as he got it by legitimate means. And you're entitled to what you've got. No more, no less.

Making a decision

First of all, Socrates would ask you to examine why you think the situation is unjust. You might think, like Aristotle, that it's because of the inequality, but that that isn't the same as injustice. You could argue for equality of opportunity, as Paine does, or for Rousseau's equality of outcome; or you could define justice, as Rawls does, as fairness, or as Nozick does, as entitlement.

I've been laid off from work, and now I find there's just not enough work to go round.

Epictetus • Machiavelli • Smith • Marx • Russell

That is bad news. You're an innocent victim of the inevitable march of progress. With all this computerization, industry needs less manpower, and with the state of the economy, companies have to keep their overheads down. It's not going to be easy trying to make ends meet. And even if you can survive financially, it's demoralizing being out of work without much hope for the future. Does it really have to be like that?

It seems that Lady Luck really isn't smiling on you at the moment. You've had the rug pulled from under you, and as well as being understandably worried, because it was through no fault of your own, you feel you have no control over your life. Which, to some extent, is true, so perhaps you should put on a brave face and adopt an attitude of stoic calm. And the person you should consult about how to do that is **Epictetus** (*c.*55–135 CE), doyen of the Stoic school of philosophers. The first thing he'd tell you is to ignore the popular misconception that Stoicism is just "grin and bear it". It's a bit more subtle than that.

He would concede, however, that there's a lot that we have no control over. You plan a picnic, but it rains. You leave your new car in the parking lot, and somebody smashes into it while you're shopping. You lose your job. But, Epictetus would tell you, these are external things which you have no power over. What really matters is the things that you do have control over, your desires and ambitions, your actions and behaviour and,

most importantly, your attitude to life. Shit happens. But so does good stuff. There's nothing you can do about that, but you can learn not to let any of it, good or bad, affect you too much. Maybe you're feeling particularly bad about losing your job, because you placed too much value on it, let it define you rather than define yourself. Concentrate on your inner values. Then no matter what life throws at you, you'll cope.

Which is fine as far as it goes, but adopting the right attitude is only one step in dealing with your present situation. According to **Niccolò Machiavelli**, Epictetus was only half right. Roughly half of what happens is out of our control, but we have the power to do something about the other half. Losing your job, for example: that's not your fault, but you can do something about it by looking at it as an opportunity. Perhaps you could retrain, for instance, and do something you've always wanted to. Or maybe it gives you the chance for a bit of revenge on your ex-employer, using your inside knowledge to set up a rival business or join a competitor.

> *"In the long-run the workman may be as necessary to his master as his master is to him, but the necessity is not so immediate"*
> Adam Smith

That might make you feel better, but if you're trying to come to terms with losing your job, it would help to know why. Now there are some conflicting opinions on the subject of what causes unemployment, so let's seek the advice of a couple of philosophers who don't exactly see eye to eye, **Adam Smith** and **Karl Marx**. While Smith would certainly sympathize with your situation, he would explain that your job was just a small cog in the machinery of the wider economy. (Marx would already be bristling at this belittling of your role.) And the economy is controlled by the laws of the market, supply and demand. Sellers produce things, and sell them for a profit, and buyers pay for the things they want and need. If production goes up, prices fall; if demand goes up, prices rise. But in the long run, everybody, buyers and sellers, benefit. Except, Marx would interject, the workers. Ah yes, Smith would concede, that is unfortunate. If there is an oversupply of labour, some workers will be laid off. But wages will go down and employers will be able to produce things more cheaply, stimulating demand, which in the long term will be good for everyone.

At this point, Marx, spluttering into his beard, would take over the conversation to put you right about things. Smith is absolutely right about the market economy, he'd tell you, but that's not an ideal way of running an economy. Quite apart from the fact that it will continually be fluctuating between boom and bust, it takes its toll on

the working class. They're treated like cogs in a machine, exploited and alienated, and when they're no longer useful, discarded. The bourgeoisie, the capitalist entrepreneurs and factory owners, benefit from having a pool of unemployed workers desperate for a job, as they can then offer them even lower wages. That's *why* you lost your job, Marx would fume, now what are you going to do about it? He'd have a few suggestions for you, most of them involving barricades and violent revolution, but perhaps when he'd calmed down would advise you to use your new-found time to become politically involved, educate yourself and others, and help to make people aware of an alternative to the unjust capitalist system.

Marx's passionate condemnation of the system may get your blood boiling, one way or the other, but it would be good to get a more measured perspective. Who

Basic philosophical question

Is some unemployment inevitable? Or can there be an economic system where everybody who wants to can work? Is work virtuous, or an unpleasant necessity? And is it immoral to be idle?

"In bourgeois society capital is independent and has individuality, while the living person is dependent and has no individuality."

Karl Marx

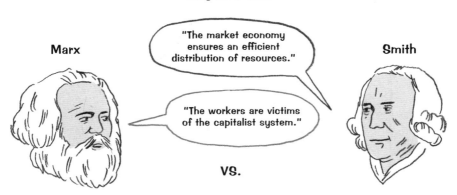

better, then, than the pipe-smoking peacenik **Bertrand Russell** (1872–1970)? He would argue that redundancies are largely caused by mechanization, and these days computerization. We've got machines now doing the work of sometimes hundreds of human workers. And more efficiently too, so production increases. So what does the employer do? Fire most of the workforce and lower the prices. Meanwhile, the workers who still have jobs are working full time, or even doing overtime. That's insane. Wouldn't it be better all round, for everybody, if the workers kept their jobs, and only worked a fraction of the hours – the extra production would cover their wages?

But no, Russell sighs, we've got this daft Protestant work ethic that tells us too much leisure is somehow sinful – especially for the working class. Work, in his opinion, is overrated. If you can survive, and don't really need to work, isn't it your duty to sit back and leave the jobs for those that want or need them? In fact, shouldn't we pay people like you to be idle, at least some of the time, if you're not too bothered about not working? That would make room for those people who really want to have a job. There's nothing sinful about being idle. And certainly nothing wrong with just sitting around thinking about things. It's what philosophers do all the time. It beats working. Try it.

Making a decision

Are you prepared to simply accept the situation, as Epictetus suggests, and get on with your life? Or should you follow Machiavelli and do something about it? You might agree with Smith that your situation is an inevitable consequence of the market economy, but at the same time rail against the system with Marx. But maybe you agree with Russell, that you can now enjoy a bit of leisure time for a while, and even consider early retirement.

Lifestyle

Chapter 3

I don't want to end up old and decrepit with no quality of life. Just give me a pill.

Bentham • Mill • Hobbes • Glover

Incurable illness or just the ravages of old age can completely destroy a person's quality of life, to the extent that there's nothing left to live for. Most people would agree – with some regret, of course – that if it was a beloved pet we were talking about, it would be better to put the poor creature out of its misery, rather than let it suffer unnecessarily. But the same rules don't seem to apply to humans, even if it's what they want for themselves. Why shouldn't we help people to die with some dignity?

It's a question that's being asked frequently these days, probably because we're all living a lot longer, and advances in medicine have meant that we can prolong life to an unprecedented extent. There are many calls for laws to permit people to have help in ending their lives if and when they reach a stage where they can no longer do it for themselves. But governments are reluctant to legalize any form of assisted suicide or euthanasia (which some denigrate as "mercy killing"), and many in the legal and medical professions have their doubts too. The debate is often emotional, or based on religious views, rather than being rational. So what would the philosophers have to say about it?

A straightforward analysis of the problem would come from **Jeremy Bentham**, the plain-speaking champion of utilitarianism. As with all moral dilemmas, he would say, this is a simple matter of deciding which of the options does the greatest good. There are only two things we need to consider, pain and pleasure, as they determine the ethically correct thing to do: maximize pleasure and minimize pain. That's utilitarianism in a nutshell. If someone is suffering, minimizing that suffering goes on the positive side of the equation, and any harm that is done goes on the negative side.

Having said that, it's not quite so simple to do in practice. How do you measure pain? Or loss of dignity? Another problem is that, if you look at the wider picture, it's not just about putting an end to someone's suffering. There is often another side to the coin. For example, helping that person to die

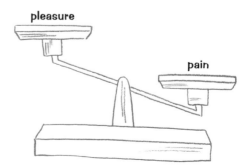

pleasure

pain

74

could also be seen as depriving her of the opportunity for pleasures in the future. And utilitarianism is about the greatest good of the greatest number of people, so we have to take into consideration other people affected by that decision. It could well be that the family and friends of the dying person would be relieved, and it may be lifting the burden of care that some have had to bear. On the other hand, there may be others who are caused distress by that person's death. Bentham would say that, although it is a straightforward question, the answer involves a complex calculation of all the possible pleasures and pains caused by that decision.

Playing God

Things wouldn't be made any simpler by Bentham's protégé **John Stuart Mill**, either. Mill went along with the basic principles of utilitarianism, but was also keen on personal liberty, so gave the idea his own slant. He would say that, because it's your own body and mind, and nobody else's, you should be free to do with them as you please, with the sole proviso that you don't harm anybody else in the process. So, if you want to take your own life, and it isn't going to hurt anybody else, that's up to you. Of course, you'd have to take into account any distress or hurt your suicide might cause, but it's still your decision. But we're getting into murkier waters when we start talking about involving someone else, in an assisted suicide, for example. There's the problem of whether someone who is effectively causing your

death, or at least being a party to it, is causing you harm by doing that. It could be argued that by giving your consent, they are carrying out your wishes, but it's still a tricky point.

The main problem, however, concerns who actually makes the decision, and who carries out the termination. If you are still able to instruct someone to help you on your way, it's different from leaving instructions well in advance, which someone else then has to decide to put into action. If you're no longer capable of ending your own life, or even telling someone else to do it, don't you put the other person into the position of "playing God"? It's one thing calmly and consciously asking a friend or doctor to give you some pills that you can decide to take or not; quite another to ask them to administer an injection. But leaving someone to die, perhaps a slow and painful death, would be to let nature take its course, so wouldn't be playing God; while giving a lethal dose of palliative drugs would. Which is preferable,

Basic philosophical question

Is assisted suicide morally justifiable?

> *"The only freedom which deserves the name, is that of pursuing our own good in our own way, so long as we do not attempt to deprive others of theirs, or impede their efforts to obtain it"*
> John Stuart Mill

though? And anyway, aren't we playing God by keeping someone alive when they would have died without our intervention?

There certainly seems to be more to this than Bentham's initial straightforward interpretation. To get another perspective, let's hear what another forthright English philosopher, **Thomas Hobbes**, might have to say. Well, for a start, he would pooh-pooh all the talk of personal liberty, and say that there have to be some hard and fast rules to make sure we're doing the right thing. If you start making concessions, or allowing exceptions, there's bound to be someone who will take advantage, and that's the beginning of a slippery slope. Once you concede that something might be morally justifiable, it creates a shift in the moral compass that leads to a whole process of moral change. It's the thin edge of the wedge.

Take euthanasia. If we allow that, we're making an exception to the rule that killing people is wrong, we're conceding that there might be circumstances when it is morally justifiable. Then we run the risk of opening the floodgates to all sorts of undesirable things: some would use the chance to get rid of a relative who has become an inconvenience, or whom they simply don't like; others would bump someone off to get at their money. There's also a serious risk that unscrupulous doctors could abuse their authority to free up a hospital bed, or help to keep within a budget; and before you know

it, some lunatic dictator could be legislating for the non-voluntary euthanasia of the disabled, the mentally ill and eventually any "inferior" people of their choosing. Worst-case scenario, of course, Hobbes would add, but it's not impossible.

On balance, Hobbes would say that the risk of a slippery slope is too great, and we should have a firm law against any form of euthanasia, even assisted suicide with the person's consent. Maybe even suicide should be made an offence to discourage people from making a decision they might have regretted, had they lived. And while we're talking about second thoughts, how about someone who, like you, has said they would like to be helped to die, and has made that clear and explicit in a "living will", but has now reached the stage where they can no longer communicate their wishes – should we assume they still want to die? How do we know they haven't changed their mind when it comes to the crunch? Or that they gave their consent to euthanasia, not because they actually wanted to die, but because they didn't want to become a burden?

Jonathan Glover (b. 1941) would ask us to look at this slippery-slope argument more carefully to see if Hobbes's fears have any foundation. Implicit in it is that the first thing you allow is morally questionable anyway, but a concession is made. But if it is shown to be acceptable, that creates a precedent which raises questions about less acceptable practices, which leads to another precedent being set, and so on. Then it gets difficult to draw the line between what is and isn't acceptable, and we start to experience unacceptable outcomes that were unintended. To avoid these unintended consequences, the position most legal and medical authorities take in the assisted suicide and voluntary euthanasia debate is to avoid making that first step.

To show that they are probably being overcautious, Glover might give the example of abortion – which arouses strong feelings both for and against. A case can be made for abortion in exceptional circumstances, however, such as when a pregnancy threatens the life of the mother, or in rape cases. But once that has been conceded, abortion has become at least sometimes acceptable, and the case can be put that it could also be justified in other circumstances, such as for foetuses that will be born disabled, or have some inherited disease. From there, the slippery-slope argument goes, it could

The slippery slope

suicide
assisted suicide
euthanasia
non-voluntary euthanasia
murder
genocide

contraception
abortion
designer babies
eugenics
infanticide

> "Nature has placed mankind under the governance of two sovereign masters, pain and pleasure. It is for them alone to point out what we ought to do, as well as to determine what we shall do"
> Jeremy Bentham

become acceptable to terminate pregnancies when the mother is incapable of caring for that child, or it will be born into a situation with risk of harm. Next thing you know, it's a form of emergency contraception, or worse, a method of eugenics.

Let's take that idea a step further. There's the question of what stage in the pregnancy abortion should be permissible. At what point does it stop being "termination" and become killing? When does life start? Where do you draw the line? Now apply that same question to the idea of abortion of severely disabled foetuses. What if the disability is only discovered at birth? If it's so severe and untreatable that the child will never have anything but suffering or would soon die a painful death, would it be the right thing to painlessly commit infanticide? What about if the problem was detected at the age of one month? Three months? Six months? It's difficult to justify aborting a severely deformed or disabled foetus without also accepting the idea of killing a disabled child. It's a slippery slope.

And so it is at the other end of life – the only difference being that an adult is able to give consent. Once we accept the idea of voluntary euthanasia, won't forms of non-voluntary euthanasia also become acceptable?

Glover thinks that that's possible, but not inevitable. Instead of thinking about what we fear might happen, he advises looking at what actually does happen when those first steps have been taken. We can look at evidence where the law has allowed assisted suicide with the person's consent, and see that it doesn't lead to a slippery slope. But it's because legislators are aware of the dangers of the slippery slope that they are very wary of introducing laws that would permit assisted suicide, and if they do, are careful to draw a very clear line to show when euthanasia, and abortion, become unjustifiable.

Making a decision:

Utilitarian philosophers such as Bentham and Mill would back you up on this, but warn that it's a more complex problem than you might think: there is much more to it than simply asking, "Whose life is it anyway?" You may, however, be swayed by Hobbes's argument that assisted suicide is the thin end of the wedge and may have unforeseen consequences, although Glover could help to allay those fears.

Is it OK to believe in homeopathy?

Hume • Aristotle • Ibn al-Haytham • Bacon • Descartes • Popper

The theory that infinitesimally small amounts of a substance can have medicinal benefit, and the smaller the dose the greater the benefit, is counterintuitive, to say the least. But there are millions of people who swear by homeopathic remedies, and even qualified doctors who prescribe them. Nevertheless, the consensus of scientists is that they have no effect whatsoever, and homeopathy is nothing more than a pseudoscience.

It sounds as if you have your doubts about homeopathy, but that you want to believe that it does what its advocates say it does. What you're really after is a method of verifying the claims for homeopathy. Well, you're in luck, because just such a method exists, and it's called science. The trouble is that not everything that claims to be science actually is science. And you can be bamboozled into believing a lot of nonsense that sounds scientific, but is really only pseudoscience because it does not follow the scientific method.

You might wonder if that really matters, and whether science is any better than belief. Philosophers would tell you that belief is OK in matters of religion, and maybe even morality, but not when dealing with the material world. Then, we have to base our ideas on evidence and our reasoning to establish the facts, not blind faith. This is the basis for science and the way it is conducted – loosely known as "the scientific method", but in fact comprising several slightly different scientific methods of testing whether a hypothesis, an idea, matches up with the facts.

You have to use a bit of common sense to understand how important science is in verifying or disproving things you might believe in. That's the advice **David Hume** (1711–76) would give you as a starting point. When somebody tells you about a miracle, you should immediately shift into sceptical mode before swallowing the story and becoming a believer. Miracles, by their very nature, defy the laws of science. What you must do is weigh up whether the fact that it breaks the laws of science is more likely than the fact that the person telling you is mistaken, or trying to mislead you. And if he's trying to sell you something, especially a miracle cure, how likely it is that it can do

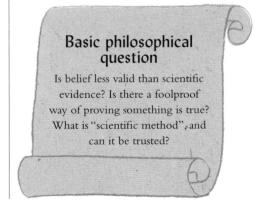

Basic philosophical question

Is belief less valid than scientific evidence? Is there a foolproof way of proving something is true? What is "scientific method", and can it be trusted?

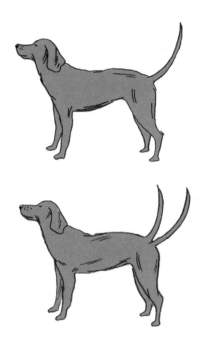

whether there seems to be any logic to it. You might notice that some things appear to follow a pattern. If, for example, you notice that when you're out fishing, everything you catch has got scales, then you can use a bit of reasoning and infer that all fish have scales. What you're doing, he would say, is establishing a general rule from lots of individual instances in the world around us. And that's something that nobody had really done before, he'd proudly tell you.

As a method of coming up with a law of nature, it could do with a bit of refining, he'd admit. There's only so much he personally could see of the world, and he had to rely on some anecdotal evidence from other observers from time to time. That might have led to one or two inaccuracies in the general rules he came up with, but he would stand by the broad principle of inferring a universal truth from a number of individual instances. And his method inspired a number of Islamic philosophers, among them **Ibn al-Haytham** (965–1039), also known as Alhazen. He admired Aristotle, and recognized he was onto something with his methodology, but al-Haytham would tell you how he realized that you need better evidence for verifying the universality of something than a few random observations and a bunch of anecdotal evidence. What you need to do, he would explain, is carry out experiments, lots of them, to see if what you think always happens really does. If you can reproduce the same results every time you do something, then you've shown that it is a universal rule.

what medical science has so far failed to do, against the likelihood that he can't be trusted.

A general rule

With that scepticism in mind, we can examine science itself and see how its trustworthiness compares with belief. The first philosopher to come to its defence is **Aristotle**, who would explain to you his method for sorting out some rules of how the world works. It's largely a matter of using reasoning, he found, of looking around at the natural world and then thinking about

> *"Truth will sooner come out from error than from confusion"*
> Francis Bacon

It was **Francis Bacon** (1561–1626) who picked up this ball and ran with it. Never one to show false modesty, he'd tell you that he developed what everybody now calls the scientific method, which is "the true way" of searching into and discovering truth, and that, until he came along, it was "as yet untried". His "Baconian method", he would explain, is to do lots of experiments to see what happens (trial and error, basically), but then – and this is the clever bit – formulate a hypothesis, come up with an explanation for what you have observed. Then you do more experiments to test whether your hypothesis is confirmed by reproducible results. If it is, hey presto, you have a scientific theory. OK, it's not that much different from what al-Haytham just said, but Bacon did formalize the whole process.

So he would tell you to suspend your belief in homeopathy until you've had the chance to get into the laboratory to test the hypothesis that tiny amounts of something can be medicinally effective. Run clinical trials, again and again, and check the results. But above all, **René Descartes** would add, be sceptical and methodical. Don't believe anything at all until you're absolutely sure you can trust the evidence beyond any doubt, and be meticulous in working step by step through the process of testing, breaking each task down into the smallest possible component bits to make sure you're doing it the same each time.

That's it. That's the scientific method. Ask a question, come up with a hypothesis, then a prediction of what you think will happen,

test it by experimentation and then analyse the results. As Aristotle said, you can establish a general rule from a number of individual instances, it's just that the idea needed a bit of fine tuning.

A bit more than that, Hume would say. There's a major flaw in this scientific method. It's based on a method of logical reasoning known as *induction*, and Hume would tell you that it doesn't prove anything. Because you're inferring a universal rule from a necessarily finite number of observations. Aristotle saw the flaw in that when he admitted that he couldn't on his own gather enough information to be sure about some things. But we never can. No matter how many times we see that, for example, when we heat pure water at sea level, it boils at

It is impossible to demonstrate that there is no Invisible Flying Spaghetti Monster, so his existence is a matter of faith, not scientific theory.

> *"Good tests kill flawed theories; we remain alive to guess again"*
> Karl Popper

100°C (212°F), we cannot say that pure water at sea level *always* boils at 100°C (212°F), because, Hume announces triumphantly, we can't observe absolutely every instance of pure water being heated at sea level. Just because the sun has risen every morning that we have any knowledge of, doesn't mean that it's impossible that it won't rise tomorrow.

That's quite a snag for science. But **Karl Popper** (1902–94) would say there is a way round this problem of induction. You'd have to change your definition of what scientific means slightly, to include the notion of what he calls "falsifiability". His idea is that a theory can be considered as scientific if it can be falsified – not that it is false, but that there is a possibility that it can be shown to be false. Your theory, arrived at by a process of scientific method, might be that every dog has a tail. You could call that a scientific theory, because it would be possible to show that it is false by finding just one instance of a dog with no tail, or a dog with two tails. On the other hand, your belief that there is an Invisible Flying Spaghetti Monster is not a scientific theory – because there's no way to prove that your claim is false, it isn't falsifiable.

And while the hypothesis that infinitesimally small amounts of a substance can have medicinal benefit is worthy of scientific investigation, as it could be shown to be false, when put to the scientific test it actually turns out to be false. So, it's not OK to believe in the efficacy of homeopathy, because it is about something that can be shown to be false, it is a scientific matter, and has indeed been shown to be false. But it is OK to believe in the Invisible Flying Spaghetti Monster if you really want to, because that's not a scientific question. The time to start doubting is when somebody says they have scientific proof of its existence.

Making a decision

Isn't it best, Hume would suggest, to maintain a healthy scepticism about all claims of cures until we have examined the evidence? Scientific method, pioneered by al-Haytham, Bacon and Descartes, among others, provides one way of critically examining "alternative" medicines such as homeopathy. You may feel, like Hume, that science itself is not infallible, but agree with Popper that some ideas can be shown to be unscientific.

My smartphone's been stolen, and I'm worried about identity theft.

Descartes • Locke • Heraclitus • Hobbes

It feels as if I've lost a part of myself, having my phone stolen like that. There was just so much of me in it – all my personal data, including bank details, medical records, passwords and so on, but also memories like my photos and emails and tweets to all my friends. And I've heard so much recently about identity theft, it scares the life out of me. To think that someone could be using all that information to pretend to be me. Now I'm beginning to doubt how I can prove I am me at all.

First of all, calm down. Losing your phone, with all that information on it, doesn't make any difference to who you are, because it's external to you, it's just a record of some of the things that make you who you are. No-one has stolen your identity, only some of the things that you associate with your identity. Although they may *be* pretending to be you, they can't be you. If I've got someone else's identity papers, I can only pretend to be them, not really be them. And the information on a phone is no better than a means of saying that the person who owns it is the person they say they are, but that doesn't mean they actually are who they say they are.

But it gets you thinking about what exactly you mean by "identity", what it is that makes you you, and not somebody else. There's obviously a lot more to it than having some ID papers, or the personal information stored in a phone or computer. The majority of philosophers and religious thinkers until about the 18th century took an understandably mystical sort of approach to the question of what makes us who we are, putting it down to what they'd call the individual's psyche or soul or spirit or mind or whatever you want to call it. Unlike your body, which undergoes all sorts of changes as you go through life, this mysterious entity is the unchanging embodiment of the true you, it is the soul (or whatever) that gives you your identity. Not everybody saw it exactly that way, as we shall see, but it wasn't until **René Descartes** came along with the notion that we are made up of a physical

Basic philosophical question

What makes me who I am? Am I the same person throughout my life, even though my body, my thoughts and ideas, and my personality change? What is it that makes me the same person at different times in my life?

> *"Everything flows and nothing stands still…*
> *you cannot step into the same river twice"*
> Heraclitus, as quoted by Plato

body and a separate, non-material mind, that some different ideas about identity emerged.

John Locke (1632–1704), for instance, would tell you not to take Descartes's theory about the separateness of the physical body from the non-physical mind too literally. Yes, of course, we've got a physical body, and in it there is a "thinking thing", but it's not what Descartes calls the mind. It's the brain. The mind is what the brain is thinking, not the thing that does the thinking. After checking that you follow him so far, Locke would move on to the next part of his argument: a lot of what is going on in our minds is processing the information we're getting from our senses. The mind, he says, is taking stuff in from our experiences of the world and then making sense of them. So, when we look at something, we are gathering information from outside ourselves, which goes from our eyes to our brain, where our mind experiences it as seeing. The sum total

of all these experiences is what makes us conscious of the world around us.

But, and here's the bit that matters, the mind also analyses that information, those experiences, and gives us a picture of ourselves in relation to them. It's this consciousness of the world and our place in it that characterizes our minds. It's also what gives us our feeling of identity. And, contrary to what Descartes and all the soul-merchants have been telling us, it is constantly changing, just as our bodies are changing, and our experiences of the world around us are changing. That's not to say that our identity changes, however, because there is a continuity to that consciousness, which is in the same mind.

Everything changes

At last, **Heraclitus** (*c.*535–475 BCE) chips in. He was beginning to think he was the only one with that sort of idea. He'd also

The teleporter

Me

probably tell you what a lonely life he'd led, shunned by almost every other philosopher, and mocked as "The Obscure" or "The Weeping Philosopher". But now Locke is vindicating what he'd been saying more than 2,000 years before. Everything changes, he'd argue. Our bodies grow up and then grow old, and our personalities and even our consciousness changes. But our identity is still the same. It's like a river that flows along, and if you step in it twice, the water is completely different the second time, but it's still the same river. Although we are constantly changing in every respect, we remain essentially the same person.

To give an analogy, he would tell you the story of Theseus's ship, which sailed the Mediterranean Sea for many years. In the course of its journeys, timber broke or rotted, and had to be replaced. By the time Theseus returned home to port not a single piece of the original ship remained. But he and his crew continued to think of it as the same ship. Were they wrong?

We now know that over the course of the years our bodies replace cells so that in time we are quite different physically, but still feel we have the same identity. And with the ease of transplant surgery, it's possible we could become biological equivalents of Theseus's ship. Locke would take issue with this,

though, and ask whether the same would apply in the case of a brain transplant...

Centuries later, **Thomas Hobbes** elaborated on Heraclitus's story and introduced a further puzzle. He asks you to imagine that all the timbers from Theseus's ship were stored as they became replaced, and some enterprising handyman used them to build a second ship, a replica of Theseus's ship. Which of the two, in your opinion, is the real ship of Theseus? And what does that make you feel about your identity? Could it in fact be stolen to make an alternative you?

Hobbes might then tell you a disturbing story that he had come across more recently,

> "*What do we mean by saying that existence precedes essence? We mean that man first of all exists, encounters himself, surges up in the world — and defines himself afterwards*"
> Jean-Paul Sartre

Other me

detail, including all the information stored in that person's brain – memories, thoughts, feelings and consciousness. At the same as it does this, the first machine painlessly destroys the original. But the person who has been "transported" is completely indistinguishable from the original, even to herself – so she believes she is the original.

If that isn't scary enough, Hobbes elaborates on this tale, too. Suppose, he says, that something goes horribly wrong; the first machine malfunctions, and the original does not get destroyed. Which of the two people is the real thing? The answer may seem obvious, because number two is demonstrably a replica that has only just come into existence, but it has a consciousness that could be said to be a continuation of number one's. And just try telling the second one she isn't who she thinks she is – she has all the credentials. Maybe you are right to be worried about your real identity being stolen after all.

a fantasy set in the near future. It involves a teleporting machine that claims to transport people across large distances instantaneously. But that's not quite the truth. What happens is a machine scans the person wanting to be transported, and then sends the information to another machine which can make an exact replica of that person, down to the finest

Making a decision

Although you needn't worry about someone literally taking your identity from you, it is difficult to pin down exactly what makes you you. You might instinctively feel that your identity is associated with your soul, psyche or mind, as Descartes describes it. Or maybe you find Heraclitus's idea appealing, that we are constantly changing, but retain the same identity. Hobbes may make you question whether someone else could have the same identity as you, but you may accept Locke's reassurance that no copy of you would have the continuity of consciousness that he says is the essential element of identity.

Will taking drugs help me understand life, the universe and everything?

Plato • Locke • Schopenhauer • Descartes • Kant • Marx

I've heard a lot from my friends about how taking mind-altering drugs is a revelatory experience. They say that some drugs can expand your consciousness, make you see things in a different way and get insights into the way the world really is. I'm not convinced. I get the impression that they just fool your brain into experiencing things that aren't real, hallucinations. That may be a pleasant way to escape from reality, but I'm not sure it helps you understand it. My friends say that you can't know what they've discovered unless you try it for yourself. Should I?

Let's make it clear before we begin that you're not asking about the ethics of taking what are probably illegal substances in your country. Your question is specifically about the possibility that certain psychoactive drugs might alter your consciousness in such a way that you go beyond your normal experience of the world, and that this experience might reveal to you things about it that you would otherwise never have access to. Right?

Now, few of the major philosophers have openly admitted to having the kind of experience you're describing, but that doesn't necessarily mean they haven't indulged. There have been rumours, for example, about where **Plato** got some of his more mystical ideas, so maybe his opinion would be a good starting point for discussion. He'd begin by expressing some sympathy with anybody wanting to find out more about the world than their senses could tell them; he too found that frustrating. It's because, he would explain, there is more to reality than what we can experience by sight, touch,

hearing, smell and taste. There's a whole world of ideas, too, and he believes that they are innate, locked away in our minds from birth. To understand this real world, rather than the illusory one we experience with our senses, we need to access those ideas somehow. His first thought, he'd say, is to get at them by reasoning, using our intellect. But now you come to mention it, it's not impossible that drugs might provide the key to unlocking those hidden ideas.

Basic philosophical question

Can we know anything more of the world than what comes from our senses? Can we trust our senses, or can they be deceived? Do mind–altering drugs enhance or distort our senses?

He would probably also make reference to his famous Allegory of the Cave (*see* page 34), where he shows how we are living in an illusory world, and if we can break free from the chains of our sensory experiences, reality comes as a revelation to us, a mind-blowing event. What isn't so clear to him, though, is whether in this analogy the drug-induced state is the illusion or the revelation. Do mind-altering substances give our senses just another illusory experience, or are they the gateway from illusion into reality? We can never know, because, like the experience of the cave-dweller who returns from the outside world to his companions in the cave, the experience of the drug-taker is seldom understood by those who haven't had it themselves, as your friends have pointed out.

On balance, though, Plato would likely say that drugs are deceptive, and the reality of the world of ideas can only be accessed by rational thinking. A silly example, perhaps, he'd say, but have you ever tried arguing

rationally with a drunk? *In vino veritas*? I don't think so. And the drugs you're talking about are not called "hallucinogenic" for nothing. They make you hallucinate, and those hallucinations are unlikely to be reliable. No more so than a dream.

No revelations

While **John Locke** would disagree with almost everything that Plato just said, he might pick up on that idea of dreaming. You see, he would argue, Plato has got it all wrong in saying that we have some mysterious innate knowledge lodged in our minds from birth. When we come into the world, we're a *tabula rasa*, a blank slate, and all we can ever know about the universe is what we experience of it. So, no matter what kind of drug you take, it's not going to magically reveal to you something that isn't there in the first place. The best it can do is deceive your senses, or at least make your brain think you're experiencing something that you're not, and that's where it's like a dream. But it can only use the information that's already in

Altered consciousness

"*No man's knowledge here can go beyond his experience*"
John Locke

> *"By wine or opium we can intensify and considerably heighten our mental powers, but as soon as the right measure of stimulus is exceeded, the effect will be exactly the opposite"*
> Arthur Schopenhauer

Deception

Halluci-nation

there, perhaps making connections that in normal circumstances it wouldn't make. That, he would maybe allow, could enable you to think about things in a different way, which might be revelatory, but surely it's more likely, given the ease with which our senses can be deceived and distorted, that that's exactly what's happening. Unless, and here he's thinking out loud, those drugs heightened your senses, or possibly let you access a sense you didn't know you had...but that would be ridiculous.

Not entirely, **Arthur Schopenhauer** would interject. Like Locke, he doubts that there is any drug that could give us any revelations that our intellects couldn't, but he does say that in his experience a number of drugs can be useful in improving our mental faculties. To a certain extent. In moderation, drugs such as caffeine, nicotine, cocaine and even alcohol and opiates sharpen our intellects so that we can reason more clearly. But take

too much and the exact opposite happens. You know, like you have a couple of drinks and it helps you to relax and get over your inhibitions, but a couple more and you're seeing pink elephants; a bit of a smoke and you can chill, but too much and you're either away in la-la land or as paranoid as hell.

But that's exactly the sort of experience that drug users are hoping for in order to experience some kind of hallucination, **René Descartes** would say. They're hoping that it will work like a deceiving demon, distorting their senses and making them believe they are in an alternative reality. In his opinion, it is an escape from reality that they're after, not any proper understanding of reality. Mind-altering drugs are essentially no different from virtual reality machines. And the clue's in the name – it's *virtual* reality, not the real deal. While that might be a welcome break from reality, would you really choose to trust it better than your non-drug-induced state to base your ideas on?

Immanuel Kant is anxious to bring this debate to a close, and in typical fashion makes no bones about saying what he thinks: what you're hoping to get from drugs is

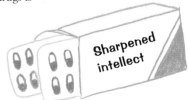

Sharpened intellect

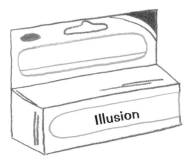

Illusion

impossible. It is, quite literally, a pipe dream. You want to get an insight into the workings of the universe, the world of things as they are, not as you perceive them with your inadequate and flawed senses. I've got news for you – you can't. You can only comprehend the phenomenal world, the world you can get information about, from your senses. There is another world, the world of the "thing-in-itself", but you can't have any knowledge of that. It's a simple as that. No ifs or buts. Drugs won't change that. They will just make you think that you can, but you can't.

You may hear atheist **Karl Marx** shouting from the sidelines at this point in the discussion. He'd remind you of his famous statement that "religion is the opium of the people", and go on to say that the analogy works both ways: the people take the opium to escape the miserable drudgery of their lives, just as they turn to religion. But aren't the revelations that come from taking drugs just as unreliable as those of religion, merely delusions we believe in because they give us some comfort?

Making a decision

You have to decide whether you think there is something "out there" that you can't experience with your senses and which will give you an insight into what the universe is really all about. Then you can ask if you can access that, as Plato believes, with your intellect, or by mind-changing substances. You might agree with Locke that our senses are already unreliable, and drugs are likely to make them more so, or with Schopenhauer that they may help to sharpen your intellect and your senses. Perhaps you think, as Descartes and Kant do, that drugs only give an illusion of revelation. But if you want to escape from miserable reality, Marx might say, why not?

If God had wanted us to be vegetarian, why did He make animals out of meat?

Aristotle • Descartes • Bentham • Singer • Eubulides of Miletus

It seems everybody these days is going vegetarian. Or even vegan. You're understandably suspicious of their motives – is it just the latest diet fad? Or are there good reasons to stop eating meat? After all, we humans are omnivores, aren't we, and like a lot of other animals, we've evolved to eat meat? It's part of the natural order of things. Yet, you would admit that we don't treat animals very well, and you'd avoid produce from cruel factory farms. So maybe the veggies have a point: animals do have some rights. But just how far down that road are you prepared to go?

Let's start by pointing out that this debate is not about animals, but about humans, and how they perceive their place in the world. It's only recently that we've come to realize that we're not the centre of the universe, and that we're part of the natural world rather than its masters. Most of our belief systems – religions, philosophy and science – have sort of taken it for granted that humans are a special case throughout much of history. So you won't find many vegans or animal rights campaigners among the philosophers until the Enlightenment, and even then they've been thin on the ground until the 20th century.

Take **Aristotle**, for instance. He spent a large part of his life travelling round the countries and islands of the eastern Mediterranean, studying the wildlife and organizing what he found into a catalogue of all living things. He had examined the different animals carefully, he would explain, and classified them according to their attributes and characteristics, and he could confirm that there is a hierarchy in nature. There are plants, which are alive but not sentient, and then there are animals. And there are lowly animals, such as worms and insects, and then there are birds and fishes and so on, and above them some more noble beasts. And at the top, naturally, are us humans.

And when the Christian philosophers came along in the Middle Ages, they used

> "*The question is not, Can they reason?,
> nor Can they talk? but, Can they suffer?*"
> Jeremy Bentham

Aristotle's hierarchy as a model for what was known as the *scala naturae*, the "Great Chain of Being", the only modification being the addition of God at the top and a few angels between Him and humankind. Medieval philosophers would tell you that it was a question of moral superiority, but also explained the food chain: plants are there for animals to eat, animals are there for other animals to eat and so on. That's why God made animals out of meat – their purpose is to provide us with food.

It was pretty much accepted that this was the God-given order of things even when scientists started to challenge religious dogmas, such as the one about the Earth being the centre of the universe. So you would find that otherwise rational philosophers, including **René Descartes**, would argue that humans are obviously superior to other life-forms. Descartes, who cleverly explained how we have a mind as well as a body (*see* page 62), was a good Catholic boy, and so used his theory to explain that it was having a mind that distinguished us from the animals. Having a mind, he would argue, is dependent on being able to think rationally. And animals don't have that power of rational thought, so they don't have minds, but are more like automata that are programmed to behave in a particular way. They can't reason, so they don't have thoughts. Therefore, they won't mind if we eat them.

If you ask **Jeremy Bentham** about that, he'd say that Descartes was asking the wrong questions. It not whether animals are capable of reasoning or not, it's whether they can suffer. And they're suffering at our hands, without any means of objecting. What's more, he argued, our treatment of them would be considered tyranny if we inflicted it on our own species. Bentham was one of the first philosophers to argue that animals aren't that different from us, and to seriously suggest that they be granted certain rights.

Basic philosophical question

Should animals have the same rights as humans? Is there a hierarchy of animals? Where do you draw the line?

"All the arguments to prove man's superiority cannot shatter this hard fact: in suffering the animals are our equals"
Peter Singer

Drawing the line

here?

here?

here?

here?

The lowest bar in this diagram is quite definitely green. And the one at the top is obviously blue. But at what point in the progression from bottom to top do the bars become blue, rather than green? Is the bar in the middle blue, or green? Or just something in between?

Drawing a line

Bentham's arguments were vindicated to some extent not long after his death with the publication of Charles Darwin's *On the Origin of Species* in 1859. Not everybody was convinced, of course, but the theory has now become accepted wisdom, and all but a few religious fundamentalists have been persuaded that we humans are simply one other organic life-form. And, according to **Peter Singer** (b. 1946), we should know our place. Just as it's sexist to assume that men are superior to women, and racist to assume that white people are superior to people of colour, assuming we're top of the evolutionary tree is an example of *speciesism*. We don't, he says, have any privilege over other species – quite the reverse: it's time that they should be given the same rights as us, to life, liberty and freedom from suffering. No more cruelty and exploitation of animals just because they can't answer back. Ban animal experimentation, and factory farming. In fact, he says, the only morally justifiable position is to become a vegan.

Hold on a second, though. Are we talking *all* animals? And if not, which animals? It might be worth consulting **Eubulides of Miletus** (4th century BCE) to examine that argument a bit more closely. He's best known for showing how difficult it can be to draw a line sometimes, like when you make a heap of sand. One grain isn't a heap. And if you add another grain, it still isn't a heap. If you keep on adding grains, when does it become a heap?

93

> *"Pythagoras, one of the oldest Philosophers in Europe, after he had travelled among the Easter nations for the sake of knowledge & conversation with their Priests & Judges seen their manners, taught his scholars that all man should be friends to all man & even to dumb beasts"*
>
> Sir Isaac Newton

Now you may not immediately see the connection, but Eubulides could make it clearer. You believe that animals suffer, so they should have rights. So, it's wrong to kill animals for sport? Yes, a majority of people think that these days. How about for food? A growing number would say yes. Do you eat fish, though? Well, yes. What about killing to control vermin, or prevent disease? Er... Now, is it wrong to club baby seals to death? Of course. How about poisoning rats? Or gassing termites? And what do you about the slugs in your veg garden? So, some animals are "superior" to others, then? Where do you draw the line when it comes to killing them? Shouldn't you be a bit more honest about whether you're making an emotional, rather than a rational, decision? And whether you really have a rational argument for killing animals for food?

It's as well to remember too that even if there is a hierarchy of animals, we are a part of it, not separate from it. And if God made all animals out of meat, we are no exception. There are many of God's creatures (crocodiles, sharks and tigers, for example) who would agree.

Making a decision

Do you think, as Aristotle and Descartes do, that humans are superior to animals? Would you agree with Descartes that non-human animals are not capable of rational thought, so can't have a mind or soul? Or maybe it's as Bentham said, not whether they can think, but whether they can suffer. If you believe that humans are simply a part of the animal world, as Singer does, then maybe you should consider stopping exploiting other animals, or even granting them some rights.

" *Because reason...*
is the only thing that makes us
men, and distinguishes
us from the beasts,
I would prefer to believe
that it exists, in its entirety,
in each of us... "

René Descartes

Sports car or station wagon?

Rousseau • Socrates • Schopenhauer • Nietzsche • de Beauvoir • Sartre
Confucius • Hume

It's time to think about getting a replacement for the trusty, but rusty, little runabout you've been driving for the last few years. Your partner thinks this is the time to get something more practical, a people carrier or minivan, for example, so obviously has a family in mind. And that will mean the prospect of hanging on to a steady job to keep up with the payments, as those things don't come cheap. But you've always hankered after a sporty two-seater, and could afford if you didn't have a family to worry about. Tough choice.

And it's similar to a lot of choices we have to make during our lives, between the sensible thing to do and the one that seems to be more attractive. Because, let's face it, it's not the cars you're having to choose between, is it? You've reached a crossroads in your life, and you've got to decide which path you're going to take. Do you go down the conventional route of career, family and camping vacations (the station–wagon option)? Or do you go for the thrill of taking on new challenges, meeting new and exciting people, and getting to see the world (the sports–car option)?

If you're seeking advice from philosophers, however, you should be warned: many of them have a poor track record when it comes to family life. It may be that, rather than making the sports-car/station-wagon choice, they've devoted their lives to the noble but financially precarious calling of philosophy. A surprising number of them (including Plato, Thomas Hobbes, John Locke, David Hume, Adam Smith, Immanuel Kant and Jeremy Bentham) not only remained unmarried, but apparently lived quite celibate lives. On the other hand, there are several whose private lives were more, let's say, complicated. In any case, whatever counsel they give you is quite likely to be of the "Do as I say, not as I do" variety – like **Jean-Jacques Rousseau**, who only grudgingly married his lover after a long

> *"Work, worry, toil and trouble are indeed the lot of almost all men their whole life long. And yet if every desire were satisfied as soon as it arose, how would men occupy their lives, how would they pass the time?"*
> Arthur Schopenhauer

> *"Even cohabitation has been corrupted – by marriage"*
> Friedrich Nietzsche

affair, and abandoned all five of his offspring, but had the cheek to write a treatise on how to bring up children.

One of the most domestically conventional, surprisingly, was **Socrates**. He was in the army as a young man and distinguished himself in active service, and on his return to Athens, married a much younger woman, with whom he had three sons. He would tell you, certainly if you were within earshot of his wife Xanthippe, to choose the station wagon. No question. Which is not like Socrates's normal approach to a philosophical problem. If you'd caught him on his own, out in the marketplace, he'd bombard you with questions to get you to see what your real dilemma is. But he might also confide in you the station-wagon idea was Xanthippe's, not his, and if he had his way he'd probably do without all the trappings of family life and spend his time chatting to young men in the town centre. Which he does anyway, whenever he gets the chance, he'd explain, but mainly to get away from Xanthippe's argumentativeness.

The road to ruin

Arthur Schopenhauer would be more honest about it. In his opinion, it doesn't really make much difference which car you go for, you'll be disappointed with either of them. He would tell you that's the tragedy of the human condition, you're always wishing for something, and either not getting it, or if you do get it, ending up disappointed with it and wanting something else. That

had been his experience anyway – a string of meaningless and unhappy love affairs, an illegitimate daughter who died as a baby, and then falling desperately in love with a young woman who rejected him. So you're better off living the life of a hermit.

You spend your life at first going out looking for fun, and when you've succeeded in doing that, you find it's not as great as you thought it would be. So you start trying to find a life partner with whom you can settle down and raise a family. Your wedding day is supposed to be the happiest of your life, but it just marks the beginning of another stage in your dissatisfaction. Along come the kids, and after the initial buzz, and the fleeting joys of their various milestones, you start looking around again for something else to long for. An affair, perhaps. But that's not going to work out as you'd planned either. Separation, divorce, loneliness, old age and impotence follow in all too rapid succession, and then you die. If you're going to use transport as

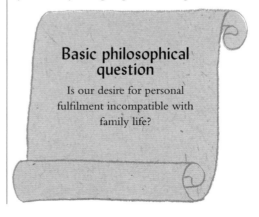

Basic philosophical question

Is our desire for personal fulfilment incompatible with family life?

a metaphor for the stages of life, he would suggest your options go something like this: stroller, scooter, tricycle, bicycle, motor bike, runabout, family saloon, people carrier, sports car, wheelchair, hearse. And the last one's the only one you don't get to feel disappointed with.

The open road

What about **Friedrich Nietzsche**, then? What would he advise you to do? His immediate reaction would be to tell you that you have to go for the sports car. Break free from the conventions, and what everybody else is telling you is the right thing to do, and dare to be different. If you don't do it now, you may never get another chance, and you'll regret it for the rest of your life. It's the option he took for himself, pushing himself to the limits without a care for what people thought of him, and without

the responsibilities of a family to hold him back. He lived life in the fast lane, he'd say, and eventually paid the price for it with nervous breakdowns and syphilis. Would he say he had any regrets, you might ask. And he might, just possibly, reveal that that lifestyle was a sort of second choice. His first choice would have been the station-wagon life, with the woman he wooed for years, but who repeatedly turned down his proposals of marriage. It could have turned out so differently, but that's life, and having chosen the sports-car option, he would recommend it to anybody.

It would be interesting to get a woman's insight into the dilemma, and who better than **Simone de Beauvoir**? Especially as she was the long-term partner of another philosopher, **Jean-Paul Sartre**. Theirs, she would explain was an "open" relationship, and she wanted neither to get married nor

> "*The superior man does what is proper to the station in which he is; he does not desire to go beyond this*"
> Confucius

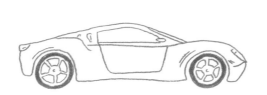

to have children. So, this gave her the space to carry on living the sports-car life with no ties, but having Jean-Paul in the background all the time was like having a station wagon in the garage in case it was ever needed. The only problem with this arrangement was that he would on occasions borrow her sports car to impress his latest squeeze, too.

This is exactly the sort of thing that **Confucius** would say you should be avoiding. Family values are the bedrock of society, and the relationships within a family are the model for how we interact with one another. So, you should not be flaunting your irresponsible lifestyle by driving a sports car, but instead be setting an example to others by proudly transporting your family in a safe and dependable station wagon.

In the final analysis, then, it's a simple question of whether you should follow your head or your heart. And you might like to bear in mind what **David Hume** (a confirmed bachelor) had to say about that: "Reason is and ought only to be the slave of the passions." So it's the sports car then!

Making a decision:

This isn't really about what kind of car you want, is it? You're deciding what kind of life you would like to lead – taking on the responsibilities of family life, or going it alone and following your dreams. You could follow in the footsteps of Confucius, Socrates and others and settle down to domestic life, or emulate Plato, Hobbes, Locke, Hume, Bentham and Kant and devote your life instead to philosophy. If you follow your heart rather than your head, you'd be taking the same route as Rousseau, Schopenhauer, de Beauvoir and Sartre – and, although he didn't plan it that way, Nietzsche.

I had a tough childhood, all right? It's not my fault I turned out bad.

Aristotle • Boethius • Nietzsche • Socrates • Bentham

Some people get a bad start in life, don't they? No money, growing up in a rough neighbourhood where kids learn to fight and steal at an early age, a poor education and then no prospect of a decent job. If anything home life is worse: abuse, violence and broken relationships. No wonder you ended up in a life of petty crime and aggressive behaviour. But did it have to be like that? Couldn't you have chosen a different path in life, despite your background?

You seem to be playing a couple of games here, in explaining the reasons for your wrongdoing. First you're looking for sympathy, which is fair enough, given your tough background, and then you're playing the blame game, which is maybe a bit harder to justify. There's a difference between finding reasons and making excuses, and although you might be able to point to the causes of your behaviour, the argument that that exonerates you from responsibility is less convincing, isn't it?

Aristotle would say that everything that happens in the world happens for a reason; there is a cause for it. Now, he'd also explain that when he talks about causes, it doesn't mean simply that when one thing happens it causes another thing to happen, like pushing a domino over and causing the next one to topple, and then the next and so on. That's just one aspect of what he's getting at. Instead, he says that the cause of something is the answer to the question "Why?" What causes that thing to come about? And he'd suggest there are four different kinds of answer to that question.

Cause and effect

First there's what Aristotle would call the "material cause", what something is made of. In your case, your material cause would be that complex combination of organic substances that we call a human being: you are who you are because of what you are, a human being. The next is the "formal cause", the way that material is put together. It is the idea that goes behind what makes something what it is: in your case, the upbringing that

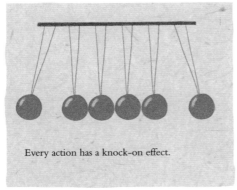

Every action has a knock-on effect.

100

you have had. Then there is the "efficient cause", which is much more like the way most people use the word cause. This refers to the external cause of something, what makes things happen or behave in a certain way, such as the first domino causing the second to fall over. In your case, it could be that somebody knocking over your drink caused you to punch him on the nose. The last cause Aristotle appropriately calls the "final cause", which is more like the purpose something exists for. A chair's "final cause" is to be something you can sit on, for example. But for you the final cause is what drives you to do what you do, your motives or desires.

Bearing that in mind, Aristotle continues, remember that every action, everything that happens, is caused by something. And that could be sheer chance, or connected to the causes he described, such as nature, compulsion, habit, reasoning, anger or appetite. Whatever it is that causes it, though, it happens as a result of something else. But here we have a problem, because whatever caused it must itself have been caused by something, and we end up with an infinite chain of events, where each thing causes the next. It's inevitable. Whatever happens is determined by what happened before. So you're entitled to blame your childhood

> ## Basic philosophical question
>
> Are we always responsible for our actions? Should wrongdoing be punished?

for your wrongdoing, and the ultimate responsibility lies with whatever caused the beginning of this infinite chain of events. The Big Bang? God?

But Aristotle is not comfortable with the idea of infinity, and especially not with the idea that everything we do is determined by something that happened before. That way you could deny all responsibility for your actions. Instead, he would suggest, we humans have the luxury of being able to choose, so we can to some extent get away from being "caused" to do something, and can also consciously cause things to happen.

There are some philosophers who would say that the last part of Aristotle's argument is a bit of cop-out, without much justification, just because he didn't like the idea of *causal determinism*, that everything is predetermined

> *"Thus every action must be due to one or other of seven causes: chance, nature, compulsion, habit, reasoning, anger or appetite"*
> Aristotle

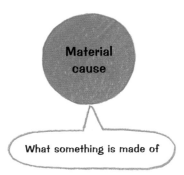

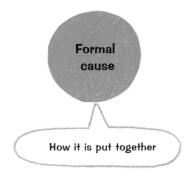

by prior events. And if you believe that, you have to accept that we are not in control of any of our actions.

Luckily, **Boethius** can offer us an answer that elaborates on Aristotle's rather weak claim that we can make choices. Part of the problem, especially in your particular case, Boethius would say, is that if our actions are predestined, then we have no responsibility for them and don't deserve to be punished if we do something wrong. What actually happens, he says, is that God (the first cause) pre-ordains everything that happens, but has also in His wisdom given us free will. That sounds impossible, but Boethius would explain that although it's all predestined, God knows what we're going to do, He can also foresee our freely chosen actions.

That's fine, if you believe in God, **Friedrich Nietzsche** would argue. But as there is no God, we are in control of determining our own actions, and by choosing our behaviour can shape our own destinies. We should not let society, our background or our past determine who we are, or what we do. We have to overcome what our past has made us into, and decide for ourselves what we can be. We have to overcome our selves! And that, he would add, means not using your tough childhood as an excuse. Face the music, and then get on with making something of your life.

In any case, the law is not interested in the problem of predestination and free will. You might be able to plead for some reduction of your sentence for mitigating circumstances, but the law doesn't allow you to pass the blame on. And that means you will face some form of punishment. You've done the crime, so you do the time.

Whether that's the right thing to do is debatable, though, according to **Socrates**.

> "*One's virtue is all that one truly has, because it is not imperilled by the vicissitudes of fortune*"
> Boethius

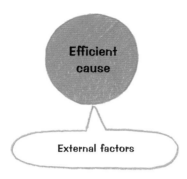

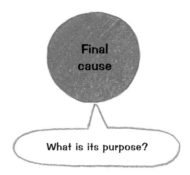

He found himself on the wrong side of the law a few times, and came to the conclusion that committing a crime is punishment in itself, as it does damage to the soul. The only possible use for punishment is if the criminal gives himself up for punishment in order to cleanse his soul. What's more, Socrates suggests that the people doing the punishment are also damaging their souls, harming themselves more than the criminal.

He'd find few backers for that argument, except among the criminal classes, you would think, but **Jeremy Bentham** broadly agrees. He would say that Socrates is right to suggest as he does that punishment is an evil, but possibly a necessary one, in some cases. That's because there are different reasons for giving punishment – for example, as retribution, or as a deterrent both to the criminal against repeat offending and to others, or as a shock to bring a criminal to his senses. It may also be simply to remove an offender from society for the safety of the people. But instead of punishment, Bentham proposes, we should be aiming to lessen crime, and that involves some sort of reform and rehabilitation of the offender. In your case, that would mean learning to see the error of your ways.

Making a decision

If you want to blame your bad behaviour on your upbringing, Aristotle would give you some support, but wouldn't completely let you off the hook. You might think, like Boethius, that all your actions are predetermined (but even he says you still have free will), or agree with Nietzsche that you should overcome your past. Whether you should be punished is another matter – it's likely that you go along with Socrates and Bentham in thinking punishment is not necessarily the solution to wrongdoing.

How do I get to be one of the good guys?

Plato • Aristotle • Machiavelli • Nietzsche

It may sound a bit schmaltzy, but I'd like to be like the good guys in those cheesy Hollywood movies. You know, the Gary Cooper or James Stewart characters, the ones who stand up for what's right against all the odds, and prove that might isn't right. They're the ones who always come out on top in the end, and are admired by everyone. Oh, and the good guy always gets the girl eventually. Not just another conquest, but real love. Seriously though, I'd like to be a good person, period. But it isn't easy to know what to do.

Life's not really like the movies, unfortunately, but you've made your point. Those are the characters who embody the things you admire, and you want to emulate them. But why? Is it because you think you're a bad person? You sound as if you're trying to be good, but you're not sure that you're doing it right. At least, not as right as all those barely believable clean-cut Gregory Peck characters. Perhaps you could pick up a few pointers from the philosophers.

And in any discussion of what it means to be good, the ancient Greeks set the agenda. Representing two differing opinions in the debate are the perennial pundits of ethics, **Plato** and his friendly rival **Aristotle**. First, let the elder of the two, Plato, give us the

benefit of his wisdom. He would explain that this is a question about the nature of virtue, the idea that embodies everything that is morally good. If you want to be good, then you have to know what virtue is. And knowing is the key here. Because, although you can't be good and do good things unless you know what virtue is, once you do know what virtue is you can't do anything but good things. In that sense, he would suggest, knowledge is virtue: you can't knowingly do bad things, because if you know what is good, you'll know why it is good, and that being good is good for you as well as everybody else, and so you'll act virtuously. To know what virtue is, you have to understand what it means. It's a sort of

> "Moral excellence comes about as a result of habit. We become just by doing just acts, temperate by doing temperate acts, brave by doing brave acts"
> Aristotle

perfection, so you won't be able find any instances of it in the world around you – nothing in this world is perfect. So virtue is an ideal, an idea that we can only think about, and it exists only in the world of ideas. The way to comprehend it, and come to know what it actually is, is to use your powers of reasoning. If you can get your head round the idea of virtue, you're on the way to becoming one of the good guys. But even then, you won't entirely match up to the ideal of being perfectly good, because that sort of perfection only exists in the world of ideas. The good guys are the ones who have understood what virtue means, and it's philosophers who use reasoning to understand the world of ideas. So, if you want to be a good guy, learn some philosophy. The philosophers are the real good guys.

Aristotle doesn't accept any of that stuff about a world of ideas. He would argue that if you want to know what a good guy is, don't sit and think about it, look around you. We get to know what anything is by seeing examples of it in the world, not in our heads. You know what dogs are like, right? That's because you've seen lots of dogs, so you know what characteristics go to make up a dog: four legs, wagging tail, barks a bit, loyalty and unconditional love, that sort of thing. It's the same with good guys. You don't have to have an idea in mind of a perfect good guy – what you do is look at all the people you know who are good guys and identify the things they do that make them

good guys: virtues such as justice, courage, tolerance, generosity. Then you can build up a picture of what being a good guy really is.

Then you'll also realize, he goes on, that those people have become good guys by doing good things. And you can do the same. You can learn to be a good guy by observing and then imitating the things that good people do, and that you and everybody else recognize as examples of good behaviour. That's how you get to be one of the good guys.

Up to no good

Now the two Athenians have had their say, it's the turn of somebody who will no doubt make you think again about your ambition to become a good guy, **Niccolò Machiavelli**. In fact, he'd come straight out with it and ask why on earth you'd want to be one of the good guys. Don't you *want* to get on in the world? All that stressing about

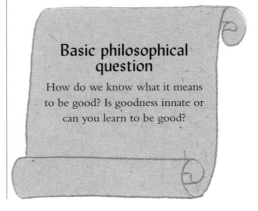

Basic philosophical question

How do we know what it means to be good? Is goodness innate or can you learn to be good?

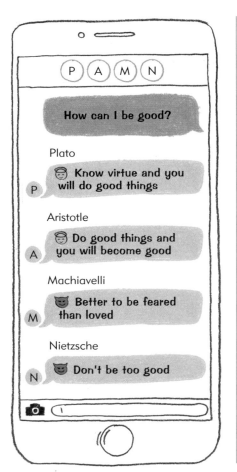

virtue isn't going to get you anywhere. It's all very well in your personal life, he'd say, but if you want to get anything done, forget it. It's not the good guys who achieve things, it's those who are prepared to ignore their own morality, and do what has to be done. In the long run, they can achieve good things too: the ends justify the means. You think those impossibly pious characters in the movies are admirable, do you? So that's why you want to be a good guy, to be admired, to be popular. Well you're in for a shock, because you don't win friends to influence people. Machiavelli would tell you that a lot of the people who come to him for advice – politicians, businessmen, that sort of person – ask him if it's better to be loved rather than feared. And the answer he gives them is that it would be nice to be both, but if you have to make a choice, it is far safer to be feared than loved.

Good guy v super man

Friedrich Nietzsche wouldn't be happy with the idea of virtue either. He'd question whether the things we've been told are virtuous, generally by religion, can be described as good at all. What's so good about being humble and weak? That's the morality of an oppressed people, slaves. And

"Behold the good and the just!…Behold the believers of all faiths! Whom do they hate most? The man who breaks their tables of values, the breaker, the lawbreaker. Yet he is the creator"
Friedrich Nietzsche

> *"If virtue is the sole good, there can be no reason against cruelty and injustice, since, as the Stoics are never tired of pointing out, cruelty and injustice afford the sufferer the best opportunities for the exercise of virtue"*
> Bertrand Russell

if we're honest, he says, that sort of thing makes wimps out of us. You can't call that "good". If, instead of holding up being meek and mild as virtuous, we consider the virtues to be such things as strength, power, ability, being good at things, good at achieving things, then we we'd revise our opinions of who the good guys are. Mild-mannered Clark Kent? No – Superman.

Think about why you want to be a good guy. Is it because you want to feel better about yourself, or you want to be admired by others? Those are pretty dubious motives, and that way you're not going to actually become one of the good guys (because it's not good to simply want to be free of guilt or to be admired), but only *appear* to be one of the good guys.

If, however, you're determined to be one of the good guys so that people like you, bear in mind Nietzsche's advice: "He who wants to set a good example must add a grain of foolishness to his virtue; then others can imitate and, at the same time, rise above the one being imitated – something which people love."

So don't be too good, it won't win you any friends.

Making a decision

You could approach this in several different ways: for example, by following Plato's method of thinking about an ideal good guy that you'd like to be, or Aristotle's method of emulating the good things people actually do. Or you might question, as Machiavelli and Nietzsche do, why you want to be a good guy in the first place, and revise your ideas of what being a good guy really means.

With all the trouble in the world today, how can I believe in God?

Epicurus • Hume • Boethius • Aristotle • Plato • St Anselm • Kant
Russell • Feuerbach • Marx • Nietzsche • Pascal

Every time you pick up a paper or switch on the news, you see stories of war, terrorism and violent crime. The world is full of people doing terrible things to each other. And while refugees are risking their lives to flee from conflict, others are profiting from their misery. It's not just what we're doing to each other, though. Natural disasters such as drought, famine and earthquakes, or dreadful diseases are killing innocent people day after day. You have to ask: why would a benevolent God let this happen?

You wouldn't be the first to ask this question. Not by a long way. The world has always been a dangerous place to live in, with people suffering and dying before their time through no fault of their own. It would be surprising if some of them didn't wonder why they were being forsaken by a God who was supposed to be so good. The idea had already been around for ages when the first philosophers started asking awkward questions in ancient Greece but, probably because they didn't want to be accused of impiety, it was quite a while before one of them actually asked the question directly.

That philosopher was **Epicurus**, the same one who gave his name to *Epicureanism*, the lifestyle philosophy of seeking out pleasure and avoiding pain. He is also credited with formulating the God and evil problem in the form of a conundrum, the *Epicurean paradox*. His reasoning went something like this: God is supposed to be omnipotent and benevolent. But evil things happen in the world. Does God want to prevent those evil

things, but isn't able to? Then He can't be omnipotent. Is He able to stop them, but not willing to? Then He isn't benevolent. And if He really is omnipotent and benevolent, where does all this evil come from?

While it doesn't explicitly give an answer to your question, it's pretty clear what Epicurus thought about the existence of an all-powerful and good God. The inference is that if an omnipotent benevolent God exists, then there wouldn't be any evil; but there patently is evil, so He doesn't exist. And it's hard to argue with that line of reasoning. Indeed, nearly 2,000 years later, the Scottish sceptic **David Hume** said in his *Dialogues concerning Natural Religion* (1779), "Epicurus's old questions are yet unanswered."

But before you jump to the conclusion that this is a watertight argument against the existence of God, bear in mind that there are lots of philosophers with a convincing line in arguments *for* His existence. Unsurprisingly, the overwhelming majority of them belong to the major monotheistic religions, such as

Judaism, Islam and especially Christianity. One of the earliest Christian philosophers, **Boethius**, even tackles the "problem of evil" raised by Epicurus's paradox. He would concede your point that there is evil in the world. But that doesn't mean that there isn't an omnipotent and benevolent God. God exists, and He is good, but in His wisdom He used His power to grant us humans free will. And because we're not perfect (like Him) we go around doing evil things.

All that sinning can't go unpunished either, so we've brought plague and pestilence and all the other nasty stuff upon ourselves. The reasoning gets a bit tortuous if you ask about the suffering of innocent people and even the good guys, but Christians would brush this off as retribution for the "original sin" we have all inherited.

Prove it

You wouldn't be alone if you weren't entirely convinced by that rebuttal of the problem of evil. Even some believers admit it is flawed. So, instead of trying to counter the argument, they have come up with their own ways of demonstrating the existence of God. There have been many different arguments put forward, but the majority of them are just variations on three main lines of reasoning.

One is the so-called "cosmological

Basic philosophical question

Can there be a benevolent God if there is evil in the world? Can we prove or disprove the existence of God? And isn't this a matter of faith rather than rational argument?

argument". This one goes back a long way, probably to the earliest Greek philosophers, but it was **Aristotle** who gave it respectability. He was a methodical, systematic man who liked to think that things happen in an orderly fashion. He would explain that nothing happens or comes into being out of the blue; there has to be a cause. And if something is caused by something else, then there must be a cause for that something else. If you take all the things in the universe, they have all come about through a chain of causes and effects, which you could, theoretically at least, trace back. Eventually, so his argument goes, you get back to a first cause, an uncaused cause, that is the origin of the entire cosmos. And that first cause, the creator of the universe, is God.

"Not without cause has one of your own followers asked, 'If God is, whence come evil things? If He is not, whence come good?'"
Boethius

Not happy with that one? Neither were a good number of philosophers, including Hume, who had a problem with assuming that just because something happens after another thing, it is necessarily caused by it. Even if we do accept that everything has a cause, isn't it a bit of a leap to argue that God is an uncaused cause? But if something caused the creator of the universe, what caused that, and...We're getting into what philosophers call an *infinite regress* here, and that's not going to answer any questions.

There's another argument based on the idea of creation that you may find more appealing. This is sometimes known as the "argument from design", or the *teleological argument* (from the Greek *telos*, meaning purpose or plan); it was advanced by **Plato** and taken up by Roman philosophers and more recently by Christian creationists (but don't let that influence your judgement). In a nutshell, Plato and his followers would tell you to look at the world around you, and marvel at the way everything is perfectly suited to its environment and, what's more, serves a purpose in relation to other things. That couldn't have happened by a random

succession of events. There is an obvious design to everything in the cosmos, a deliberate plan. And because this is evidence of an *intelligent design*, it must have a designer, God.

Still not convinced? Perhaps you would prefer the argument **St Anselm** (1033–1109) put forward. Using the *ontological argument* (from *ontology*, the branch of philosophy concerned with the nature of being), Anselm would ask you to imagine the most perfect being possible. The only element of perfection that this being lacks is existence – it only exists in your mind. So, he says, it is not the most perfect being possible, because one that does exist would be more perfect. Anselm's definition of God is "that than which nothing greater can be conceived", and to be the greatest possible being that we can conceive, it would have to have the attribute of existence. So God must exist.

A question of faith

Naturally, subsequent philosophers have come along determined to demolish these arguments, and to some extent succeeded, but you'd get a more thoughtful and constructive appraisal of them from **Immanuel Kant**. The agnostic's answer, if you like. After careful examination, he said, you'll find none of these arguments are really logically sound. You'd do far better to stop trying to prove the existence of God, because if there is a God, He's beyond our powers of comprehension, and it's a matter of faith whether you believe in Him or not,

> *"When I say that I cannot prove that there is not a God, I ought to add equally that I cannot prove that there are not the Homeric gods"*
> Bertrand Russell

not rational argument. And that view gets a witty endorsement from **Bertrand Russell** who points out that it's fairly pointless trying to prove the non-existence of something too. He'd tell you he believes there's an invisible teapot orbiting the sun, and invite you to prove him wrong. The tongue-in-cheek Pastafarian religion is based on a similar argument for the existence of the Flying Spaghetti Monster (*see* page 82).

That doesn't stop atheist philosophers from airing their views, however, and from the 19th century onwards many of them have. Most of them agree with **Ludwig Feuerbach** (1804–72) that God is a human invention, a projection of all our hopes and fears. **Karl Marx** even dismissed religion as a symptom of a sick society, rather than a comfort, and less still a solution to our woes. But **Friedrich Nietzsche** really had it in for God, and this time it was personal.

His dad was a Lutheran pastor, and young Friedrich was a devout believer until Nietzsche senior was taken ill and died a slow and very painful death. Following that, Nietzsche's answer was simple and to the point: God is dead. And we murdered Him. No way can there be a perfectly good God. What's more, we'd be daft to go on basing our morality, our ideas of what good is, on that concept.

While you're making up your mind on this one, though, you might like to mull over a thought from **Blaise Pascal** (1623–62). Think of it as Pascal's Wager, with your life as the stakes. If God exists, and you believe in Him, you stand to win eternal bliss, or something equally good. If He exists and you don't believe in Him, you face eternal damnation. Of course, if He doesn't exist it will make no difference, whatever's in store for you. What's your best option?

Making a decision

At the moment, you're one of the doubters, like Epicurus and Hume, who see a disconnect between an omnipotent, benevolent God and the state of the world. You might find some comfort in the arguments of the believers, such as Aristotle, Plato and St Anselm. Or you may think Kant and Russell have the right idea in saying that there's no real proof either way for the existence of God. If your faith is truly shattered though, you'd be in good company, along with Feuerbach, Marx and Nietzsche.

I'm scared of dying. Is that normal?

Buddha • Socrates • Plato • Zhuangzi • Epicurus • Schopenhauer • Camus

Coming to terms with your own mortality is not easy. Death is the second most significant event in your life, after birth. Every one of us has to experience it sooner or later, but because nobody survives to tell you what it's like, it remains life's great unknown. Probably for that reason, it is natural that you should feel apprehensive at the very least. But is it really something that you should be frightened of? And if fear of dying is spoiling your enjoyment of life, perhaps you should find a way of getting over it.

A lot of people turn to religion, rather than philosophy, for reassurance about death. There are no atheists in foxholes, so they say. Most religions assure us that we have immortal souls that survive after our physical bodies have mouldered away, and death is not the end, but just a stage on our journey into an eternal afterlife. But if you subscribe to any of the mainstream religions, you'll soon find out there are terms and conditions. And, far from calming your apprehension, they are more likely to put the fear of God in you. In a nutshell, most of them tell you that if

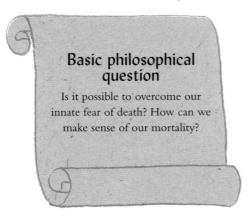

Basic philosophical question

Is it possible to overcome our innate fear of death? How can we make sense of our mortality?

you've been good, there's nothing to worry about, but if you've been foolish enough to give in to temptation...well, it doesn't bear thinking about.

Not much consolation for most of us, then. The idea that you get what's coming to you when you die runs deep in almost every culture, but there are some philosophers who have tried to soften the blow. **Buddha** (who was more of a philosopher than a religious leader, if you think about it) was brought up to believe in a constant cycle of death and rebirth, but argued that if you manage to get one of those lives right, you'll see the light. Which will promptly be extinguished, as you enter a state of *nirvana*, not-being, an end to all life and death. You might not find that reassuring, but at least with Buddhism, you get another shot at it if you mess up in life.

Not so bad

Socrates took a much more pragmatic approach to the business of dying. He had made a nuisance of himself with the Athenian bigwigs by questioning anything and everything, and ended up charged with

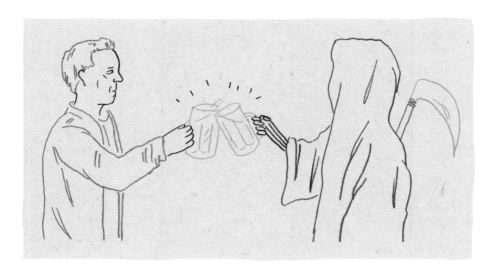

impiety and corrupting the young. Rather than giving in and shutting up, he declared, "For a human, the unexamined life is not worth living", and killed himself by drinking hemlock. So, although he clearly would have preferred to stick around asking awkward questions, he wasn't afraid of ending it all. What advice would he give about being afraid of dying, then? Well, he'd tell you that he didn't know if there was an afterlife or not. But, either way, it seemed to him that death is a good state to be in. If you believe what people say, then if you've been virtuous, you'll be going to a better place, where you will live eternally in comfort. And if there isn't an afterlife, you'll have the satisfaction of having led a good life, and get to have a good long rest.

And with that hopeful message, Socrates raised his cup of hemlock in a toast of farewell to his friends. Among them was **Plato**, who faithfully recorded the old man's thoughts, and was naturally deeply affected by his death. So much so that it is probably best you don't consult him about your morbid fears. It seems he didn't get the message from his mentor about living a good life and cheerfully going into the next one when your time came. Instead, Plato (not renowned for his sense of fun) tended to dwell on the question of mortality, and maintained that a thinking person really

"Be of good cheer about death…no evil can happen to a good man, either in life or after death"
Socrates, in Plato's *Apology of Socrates*

should be concerned about death, and meditate on it constantly. And that's probably what got you into the state you're in in the first place.

It could be, though, that it's the not knowing that's causing your anxiety. Maybe **Zhuangzi** could help you get over your fear of the unknown. He'd tell you about the time he saw a skull on the roadside, and said how sorry he was for the person who had died. The skull replied, "How do you know it's bad to be dead?" And if you're frightened of dying, more than what happens afterward, Zhuangzi would tell you that's it's just a transformation of matter from one state to another, a bit like other stages in our lives.

To an extent, **Epicurus** would go along with that. You want to know what happens when we die? The atoms that make up our bodies disperse and reform as something else, somewhere else in the universe. But that's it, according to him. No more life, no more consciousness. Nothing – full stop. And that, he would point out, is something you should be grateful for, not frightened of. Death is an end to our bodies and our consciousness, so it's an end to our pains and fears too. You don't have to worry about death, because as long as you're alive, death doesn't exist for you, and when death comes, you don't exist. That's not to say that he would welcome death – quite the opposite. Unlike his Stoic

contemporaries, who continually talked up death as something heroic and honourable, he thought that dying, the absolute end of our being, is the worst thing that can happen to us. But being dead? That's nothing.

The meaning of death

Generally the least likely philosopher to offer any reassurance, **Arthur Schopenhauer** does however offer some crumbs of comfort about death, albeit in his characteristically bleak manner. In his opinion, life is just one long, pointless series of sufferings, so the alternative is not likely to be any worse. Anyway, why are you so concerned about what happens after your death? Isn't it the same as before you came into existence? You've already spent an eternity not existing, so it shouldn't hold any terror for you. Just stop speculating about it and get on with the misery of life instead.

Or not. The trouble with thinking about life is that you'll inevitably end up facing your own mortality again, the realization that you actually exist, and will cease to exist. That *existential crisis*, as the trendy French existentialists called it, is a sobering thought. Or maybe exhilarating. And quite possibly terrifying. In answer to your original question: yes, it's quite normal to be afraid of dying. But also to be afraid of living. Because

> "No evil is honourable; but death is honourable; therefore death is not evil"
> Zeno of Citium, as quoted by Seneca the Younger

> *"Death, therefore, the most awful of evils,*
> *is nothing to us, seeing that, when we are, death is not come,*
> *and, when death is come, we are not"*
> Epicurus

you have to ask: what's the meaning of life – no, is there a meaning to life? **Albert Camus** (1913–60) (who comes a close second to Schopenhauer in the contest for gloomiest philosopher of all time) would warn you that it's futile trying to make sense of our mortality, or trying to find a meaning in life. You're born, you live, you die. That's it. It's all pretty pointless, really, so you might as well overcome your fear of dying and think about ending it all now. Then you won't have to face up to that fear and angst any more. Now, in case you think that's a bit nihilistic (which, let's be honest, it is), he'd tell you that suicide is actually a cop-out – but now you've contemplated it, you've confronted your fear of death. And now you've done that, wouldn't it be better to get on with life, but accept that it is meaningless, or even a bit of a joke in very poor taste? To prove the point, Camus's own life as a philosopher, footballer and Nobel-prize-winning novelist, was pointlessly cut short by a car accident when he took a lift from a friend and threw away the train ticket he had just bought. That's life.

Making a decision

Although most people have a fear of dying, philosophers can offer some comfort. You might be reassured by Socrates's idea that you're going to a better place, or at least the notion put forward by Epicurus, Buddha and Schopenhauer that it will be an end to your suffering. But if you're still dwelling on thoughts of death and dying, as Plato thought you ought to do, you might end up agreeing with Camus that it will help you come to terms with the absurdity of life.

Leisure

Chapter 4

Why does everybody take things so seriously? I just want to have a good time.

Socrates • Diogenes of Sinope • Epicurus • Schopenhauer • Buddha
Aristotle • Nietzsche

Why can't people just lighten up? There's plenty to be miserable about already, so why dwell on it? And I'm fed up with moralizing spoilsports who constantly tell me that whatever I think is fun is either shallow, immoral or bad for me. It's not hurting them if I have a good time, so why should I worry? If they enjoy agonizing over what's right and wrong, that's up to them, but I think life's too short for all that.

Fair enough. It's your life, and you naturally want to do whatever makes you happy. The question is, however, what do you think makes you happy? What do you mean by "having a good time"? From the way you're talking, it looks as if you mean enjoying the sensual pleasures of sex and drugs and rock 'n' roll, without having to think too much about what you're doing. That's what a lot of people would like, given the chance. The good life.

Now that, "the good life", is something that philosophers through the ages have discussed at length. Maybe that just reinforces your view that they're taking it too seriously, instead of getting out there and enjoying themselves. But bear with them, because they want to find out what really does make us happy, so that we can all get the most out of life. For the ancient Greeks, for example, the goal was what they called *eudaimonia*, which loosely means happiness, but more specifically "good spirit", or feeling good. But the debate centred on identifying what

we should do to make us feel good.

It depends, of course, on what you mean by "good". Do you mean good as in a good cigar? Or as in a good person? There's a difference between something being pleasurable, and something being virtuous, but we would describe them both as good. So, **Socrates** would ask, what do we mean by "the good life"? Pleasure or virtue? This is just the sort of topic that would set him off on a seemingly endless series of questions, trying to winkle out what you mean by having a good time, and showing that you might not have thought it through yet.

Happy or virtuous

Socrates might ask you to consider two men, one who tries to do what is morally right all the time, the other who seeks pleasure in everything he does. Let's call them Mr D. and Mr E., respectively. Now, take Mr D. Would you say he's a good man? Yes, he's renowned for it. Why? Because he does good things. Is that what you mean by having a good time?

> *"The unexamined life is not worth living"*
> Socrates, quoted by Plato

No, of course it isn't. But you'd say that he is leading a good life. Why is that different from having a good time? Because it's a different kind of "good". Is it because what you mean is he is leading a virtuous life? Now we're getting to the heart of the matter. Is a virtuous life different from a good life, then?

Before you answer that, look at Mr E. Is he having a good time? Yes, it would appear so, as he's eating, drinking and enjoying sensual pleasures. That's a good thing, is it? You don't seem so sure about that. Perhaps you mean it's a pleasurable thing, then, it makes him happy. So good things are things that make you happy? That seems to be what you're saying.

Let's go back to Mr D. Is he happy? He certainly seems to be. But is he satisfying his physical desires? Not really – if anything, he's trying to ignore them. So what is making him happy? Is it because he is doing good things, virtuous things? Now, being happy is the same as what you would call having a good time, isn't it? So he's having a good time, a pleasurable time. And if you can have a pleasurable time by doing virtuous things, isn't that better than having a pleasurable time doing things that are not virtuous?

It's likely Socrates would smile at your confusion, and maybe even laugh, pointing out that he's happy with the way the debate has gone. He'd tell you how much he enjoys that sort of intellectual conversation, and that people who don't have them are missing out on a lot of pleasure. Just going after sensual satisfaction is skimming the surface of life,

and rather than "the good life", it's a pretty shallow existence. He'd then say that he had a good time talking to you, and now was off for a good lunch and a glass of wine.

As well as making your opinion look shallow and simplistic, Socrates laid out the two opposing sides of the argument, using Mr D. and Mr E. Who could easily be **Diogenes of Sinope** (*c.*404–323 BCE) and **Epicurus**. Epicurus would tell you that pleasure, whether that is sensual pleasure or intellectual pleasure or just feeling good about doing things, is nature's way of telling that something is good, and pain or suffering that it is bad. So go ahead, he would say, and have a good time, but as Socrates suggested, don't think that always means indulging in the pleasures of the flesh.

Diogenes, on the other hand, would tell you to forego all those ephemeral pleasures and strive for the deeper ones of living to a strict moral code. Lead a simple, or even spartan life, in harmony with nature. And that

Basic philosophical question

What is "the good life"? How does it differ from "having a good time"? Does true happiness come from pursuing pleasure, or virtue?

A middle way

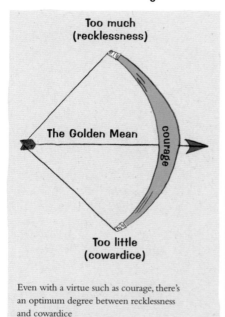

Too much (recklessness)

The Golden Mean

courage

Too little (cowardice)

Even with a virtue such as courage, there's an optimum degree between recklessness and cowardice

means taking the rough with the smooth, accepting that sometimes the sun shines, and sometimes it rains, and there's nothing you can do about that. So you won't always be able to achieve your desires, and should instead just content yourself with satisfying your basic physical needs. In any case, most of our dissatisfaction comes from always trying to have a good time, instead of leading a good life.

Arthur Schopenhauer would pick up on that idea of failing to achieve your desires. In typically pessimistic fashion, he'd tell you

that, if you just want to have a good time, you're going to be bitterly disappointed. Diogenes got it half right – if you want something that's out of reach, you'll be disappointed – but what he didn't say is that even if you do get it, it almost certainly won't satisfy you, or at least not for long. And once you've had your fun, what next? You'll be itching for more. Which is likewise doomed to failure. We're condemned to a life of suffering, resulting from our continual disappointment and frustration in trying to satisfy our desires, and especially the desire to be happy. Forget it. You won't be, even if you have what you think is a good time.

The middle way

That's pretty much the view of Siddhartha Gautama, the **Buddha**, but the tranquil smile on his face hints that he has an answer to that, that he has the secret to leading a happy life. He'd tell you that he spent his early years living the life of a prince, enjoying all the luxuries you could possible imagine, but found no real satisfaction in them. He decided then to take up the life of the ascetic, pursuing nothing but spiritual goals. And nearly starved to death. It was at this point that he achieved enlightenment, he explains, and realized that there was a middle way. You'll never satisfy your desires for sensual pleasure, but there's no point in denying them. You'd do better to acknowledge that they exist, and then try to overcome them.

Isn't that similar to what Socrates was trying to get you to say, too? That there's a middle way between a life of virtue and a life

> *"The mother of excess is not joy but joylessness"*
> Friedrich Nietzsche

of pleasure? **Aristotle** would go along with that idea, and rather than calling it a middle way, he described it is the *golden mean*. There has to be moderation in all things, he'd argue, and that goes for virtue too. The golden mean, according to Aristotle, is that ideal point between excess and restraint. If you take a virtue such as courage, for example, it can be overdone. Someone who shows too much courage has strayed into the realms of recklessness, which cannot be considered virtuous. And someone who shows too little courage is guilty of cowardice, again not in any way a desirable trait. And so it is with everything in life, finding the golden mean between going too far and not going far enough. So have a good time, by all means, but not too good, and be good too, but not too good.

Friedrich Nietzsche wouldn't be so happy with that idea, given his disdain for conventional morality, but would drag the argument away from virtue and back to the idea of satisfaction. Forget whether what you're doing is morally good, and concentrate on achieving something, he says. But don't just go for the easy pleasures: they're not as good as you think they will be. Schopenhauer is wrong to suggest that you can't satisfy your desires. You can, if you dare to try. And the degree of satisfaction is dependent on the amount of struggle you put in to achieving what you desire. Just as there's no virtue in dismissing your desires, there's no virtue in hard work and pain for its own sake – there has to be a reward at the end of it. For example, the view from the top of a mountain can be breathtaking, but if you climbed that mountain, you'd appreciate it more than someone who got there by helicopter. And when you look back on your life, like admiring the view from the mountain, would you rather say that you had a good time, or that you had a good life?

Making a decision

Before rushing to a decision, you could take Socrates's advice and ask yourself exactly what you mean by "a good time". Do you mean happiness, as in satisfaction of your desires and sensual pleasure, as Epicurus might put it? Or do you mean a virtuous life, in accord with nature, as described by Diogenes of Sinope? Or is there a middle way, like the one advocated by Buddha and Aristotle? Or maybe Nietzsche's got it right, saying that a good life is one in which you have achieved your potential.

My family want to go camping – but I can think of nothing worse than getting "back to nature".

Diogenes of Sinope • Pythagorus • Lao Tzu • Confucius • Hobbes • Rousseau • Schelling Thoreau • Emerson • Naess

The idea's good – getting in touch with the natural world, living life as it ought to be lived, the "good life", if only for a brief time. But the reality is much less attractive: day after day of battling against the hostile elements and voracious insects, struggling to produce barely edible meals over an open fire and snatching a few hours' sleep in an uncomfortable bed. Sure, the countryside is beautiful, when you can see it through the rain, but it's small consolation. Would any civilized philosopher recommend camping?

Well, yes. In fact, a sizeable majority of philosophers through the ages would side with your family, and wax lyrical about the virtues of the natural world. How many of those would actually join you on a camping trip is another matter, though. Philosophy is a product of civilization, the process of establishing societies in towns and cities, and philosophers for the most part are urban creatures with the luxury of time to think. And when they do think about it, they overlook the drawbacks of rural life, and dwell on an idealized notion of nature as a model for the "good life", life as it ought to be lived.

For most of them, it's a case of do as I say, not as I do. The Cynics, for example, came up with a philosophy based on living in harmony with nature, while living themselves in all the comfort of prosperous Athens. An honourable exception was **Diogenes of Sinope**, also known as Diogenes the Cynic (from the Greek word for dog, because he lived like one), who actually practised what he preached. He took the back-to-nature idea very seriously, and to make his point lived in a tub in the marketplace in Athens, and performed all his natural functions in the open. He would definitely approve of your camping trip, but would recommend it as a permanent change rather than a break from everyday life.

Basic philosophical question

Should we be trying to live in harmony with nature, or to transcend it? Are our ideas of the "good life" and beauty derived from nature? Or do we project our ideas onto nature?

Diogenes was an inspiration to other Cynic philosophers, and the Stoics who later took up the mantle of finding virtue in natural living. But for all the talk of how wonderful nature is, the Greeks were only keen on their own idealized version of it. From **Pythagoras** (*c.*570–495 BCE) onwards, they saw in it what they wanted to see: order, balance, symmetry and elegance. This was reflected in their art and architecture, which classical Greek urbanites seemed to prefer to its original inspiration. Plato saw the study of nature as an exercise in geometry, and Aristotle spent most of his life trying to get the natural world to fit his classification. They'd certainly think the camping trip is a good idea, but don't go without all the modern equipment.

Law of the jungle

If you're looking for support for your case against a holiday in the country, you might do better to turn to the East. Like Greece, the ancient Chinese civilizations spawned a back-to-nature movement, Daoism, led by the possibly mythical Lao Tzu, who maintained the good life consisted of following the *dao*, "the way", the force behind all of creation,

"In all things of nature there is something of the marvellous"
Aristotle

its very essence. But China also gave us **Confucius**. He would sympathize with your misgivings about venturing into the countryside. The landscape is beautiful, he would admit, and especially as a subject for artistic inspiration, but only if you leave out the unattractive bits, and imbue it with the elegance and sophistication that it lacks. Confucius devoted his career to creating a cultured civil society based on respect for our fellow humans, far superior to the old rustic way of life. Having gone to the trouble of making life more civilized, why on earth would he want to go back to living like a country hick, even for a short time?

That was a view echoed by **Thomas Hobbes.** The England he lived in was prosperous and comfortable, thanks to the civilizing efforts of "that Rationall and most excellent worke of Nature, *Man*". But he was under no illusions about what nature was really like; strip back the veneer of civilization, and you see how people behave in a "state of nature". It's not pretty. Everything in the natural world, he would tell you, is battling for existence. Nature, "red in tooth and claw" as Tennyson later put it, is something we should be constantly trying to overcome, so that we don't have to struggle to survive the law of the jungle. Hobbes would seriously question how "Rationall" it

is to contemplate any leisure time spent in such a "poore, nasty, brutish" environment.

You might think that as society has become more urbanized and prosperous, people would shun the idea of getting back to nature. Far from it. It seems that the more civilized we become the more we hanker after a lost rural idyll. The rot set in with **Jean-Jacques Rousseau** with his revolutionary idea that everything natural is good, but is corrupted by civilization. It was the start of a backlash against Enlightenment sophistication, urbanization and rationality, with new Romantic ideas about seeking inspiration from the natural world. City folk flocked to the country in their leisure time to enjoy the delights of nature, starting a fashion that continues to your family's present desire for a camping holiday.

Enthusiasm for getting back to nature spread to Romantic artists, writers, musicians and even philosophers. For about a century, nature was the touchstone for the predominant German Idealist philosophy, and just about every German philosopher was an advocate of trips to the country. Perhaps the most ardent admirer of all things natural was **Friedrich Schelling** (1775–1854), who described man's oneness with the total reality that is nature. No need to ask where he would stand in the camping debate. Nor

"All natural objects make a kindred impression, when the mind is open to their influence. Nature never wears a mean appearance"
Ralph Waldo Emerson

> *"Oh providence! Oh nature! Treasure of the poor, resource of the unfortunate. The person who feels, knows your holy laws and trusts them, the person whose heart is at peace and whose body does not suffer, thanks to you is not entirely prey to adversity"*
>
> Jean-Jacques Rousseau

would you have any doubts about what the New England Transcendentalists, **Henry Thoreau** (1817–62) and **Ralph Waldo Emerson** (1803–82), thought about your reluctance to engage with nature. They turned their backs on city life completely, in favour of the log cabin in the woods, such as the one described in Thoreau's *Walden*, and sparked off an interest in developing a philosophy that has the natural environment at its heart.

Deep green

A green philosophy known as "deep ecology" (to distinguish it from the "shallow", anthropocentric branch of the science) emerged from the work of Norwegian philosopher **Arne Naess** (1912–2009). He argued that we humans are merely a part of the whole natural biosystem, and that we should therefore learn to live within it, rather than constantly trying to tame it to our own ends; we should also think about the long-term effects of our actions on nature as a whole. Perhaps the most realistic of the philosophers you might consult on the issue, let's allow Naess the final say on the wisdom of your family's camping trip. While he might have sneered slightly at the idea of a camping holiday as only a temporary break from a destructive urban lifestyle, he would certainly prefer you did that than hop on a plane to a concrete blot on the natural landscape.

Making a decision

If you're looking for reassurance that you might actually enjoy at least some aspects of a camping holiday, you could take the advice of Lao Tzu, or Diogenes of Sinope. However, the other Greek philosophers, and later Romantics such as Schelling, had a rather idealized concept of "Nature", which is perhaps less convincing. While Hobbes provides an argument against the nastiness of nature, Rousseau extols its virtues, and Thoreau and Emerson point out the flaws of urban life. Even if you are an inveterate urbanite, suspicious of Romantic notions of Mother Nature, perhaps a change would be as good as a rest...and Naess argues you'd be helping to save the planet.

Should I worry about how my food is produced?

Epicurus • Diogenes of Sinope • Geber • Marx • Naess

When you sit down to have a meal, you're looking forward to enjoying something tasty, and a chance to relax. But there's always the nagging doubt that what we enjoy eating isn't good for us, or the planet. It's not just the junk food we indulge in from time to time. Agriculture and the food industry are big business these days, and the goods we buy from the supermarket are often full of additives, and produced to make profits rather than with the consumers' best interests in mind. Of course, you'd like to eat healthy, fresh food, but it's often a matter of price and convenience.

It's a decision most of us make at one time or another, opting to buy ready-prepared, pre-packed or processed food, rather than getting fresh ingredients from the grocer or the farmer's market. But why should we feel guilty about it? We normally reserve any feelings of guilt for moral issues, so there must be something ethically wrong with the notion of convenience food, and not just whether it's bad for us.

Of course, there's the whole issue of whether or not the food we get from the supermarket is nutritious and healthy, or if it is actually doing us harm. Now we're talking values, and can see why you might suffer a pang of guilt with your choice of taking an easy option that you know is of dubious merit. And that's where the philosophers would be eager to advise you.

Given his reputation for choosing anything that gives us pleasure, and avoiding anything that is unpleasant, you'd expect **Epicurus** to plump for whatever gives you the greatest enjoyment, and involves the least hassle, no matter what its provenance. But if you asked him, he wouldn't be as quick as you might have thought to recommend an indulgent plateful of what you fancy. He'd say there's a good case for getting a ready-prepared meal, for example, rather than having to go through the chore of preparing a meal for yourself, and he'd also admit that there's a sort of sinful pleasure in eating stuff you know isn't good for you, but is rather delicious.

On the other hand, though, looking at the

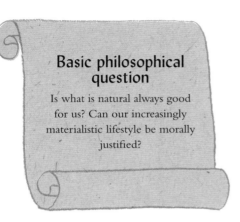

Basic philosophical question

Is what is natural always good for us? Can our increasingly materialistic lifestyle be morally justified?

bigger picture, he's always said that an excess of anything has the opposite effect to what we were looking for. Too much rich food, and you end up getting indigestion. And too much junk food will make you fat, spotty and flatulent, which isn't what you would call pleasant. While convenience food is, well, convenient, and may give you some fleeting pleasure, it's unlikely to be nutritious and quite possibly harmful if taken in large doses or over a period of time. It's not called junk food for no reason. So, by all means, indulge yourself now and again, but don't make a habit of it.

A thumbs-up from Epicurus, then, if a hesitant one. There's no such endorsement from **Diogenes of Sinope**, however. He brings the question down to a simple matter of whether you think it's better to eat a sugar-, salt- and fat-filled feast, seasoned with preservatives and colourings, or a nutritious bowl of lentils and a salad. It really is that simple, in his opinion. Our ancestors, not that long ago, were hunter-gatherers, and we should be living in harmony with nature and

eating the diet nature designed us for. It's just not natural for us to fill ourselves with all that processed junk, which is no doubt laced with a cocktail of chemical additives.

Health food

At this point in the discussion, Abu Mūsā Jābir ibn Hayyān (c.8th century CE), who is known more conveniently in the West as Geber, would politely interrupt. He'd point out that, as a practising physician and pharmacist as well as a philosopher, he is perhaps better qualified than Diogenes to speak about the nutritional pros and cons of different diets. The use of words such as "natural" and "chemical" in that argument, he'd respectfully suggest, is a load of camel manure. He'd explain that he'd noticed that some people die from eating "natural" poisonous plants such as hemlock, so just being natural doesn't mean it's good for you. Nor does something that is man-made necessarily have to be harmful: a lot of the medicines he administers were concocted in his laboratory, and don't occur in nature. So why should living in accord with nature be so good? You could say that it's "natural" to

die in our thirties (that's what happened to our ancestors), but what's so good about that?

As for the complaint that they're full of "chemicals"...his pioneering research in the science of chemistry shows that everything (yes, everything) is made out of "chemicals". Pure water is made out of the elements of hydrogen and oxygen ("chemicals"), and naturally occurring spring water contains a heady mix of other minerals and organic chemicals too.

Having said that, Geber would admit that convenience foods often are unhealthy – not because they're man-made, but because the balance of good and bad stuff in them is all wrong. It's possible that a pill invented by a good nutritionist could provide us with a properly balanced diet, better than any other kind of food, "natural" or not. And if you object to that, your argument isn't really about nutrition at all.

Grudgingly, Diogenes might concede the point, but would insist his argument about living in harmony with nature is still valid. We're basically hunter-gatherers, so it's not in our nature to have stuff handed to us on a plate, so to speak. The trouble with living in a prosperous society is that it encourages us to be lazy, to just pick up processed and ready-prepared food without a thought for how it was produced. That, he says, is ultimately demoralizing, as we are robbed of the satisfaction of sourcing and preparing the food for ourselves.

And isn't there something immoral about having the luxury of getting someone else to do the work for you, while you sit back and enjoy a surfeit of food, when this is at the cost of people who can't afford a simple nutritious meal? Diogenes would be looking to **Karl Marx** for approval. Which of course he gets, and Marx follows it up with the argument that all those processed foods may be bad for you, but that's not the point. They're bad for society as a whole, and the working class in particular. The producers of this convenience food, the bourgeoisie, are exploiting their workers to line their own pockets. And the mega-corporations that own the supermarkets are exploiting their suppliers, especially small farmers in developing countries. Their only concern is to make money, instead of producing food for the common good, and they control production of the necessities of life, which should be distributed according to need.

By buying this convenience food, you're perpetuating the system: the money goes to

> "*Luxurious food and drinks in no way protect you from harm. Wealth beyond what is natural is no more use than an overflowing container. Real value is not generated by theatres, and baths, perfumes or ointments, but by philosophy*"
> Epicurus

> When asked what was the proper time for lunch, he said,
> *"If a rich man, when you will; if a poor man, when you can."*
> Diogenes of Sinope, quoted by Diogenes Laërtius

the rich capitalists, who keep the proletariat working, producing more food to feed the poor, and make the rich richer. And what do they do with all that money? They can't eat it, can they? It's wasted on luxury items, when it could relieve all the hunger and poverty there is in the world. And the rich corporations get richer too, enabling them to take over even more of the agricultural resources, and to monopolize production by patenting GM crops, forcing the workers to rely on them to earn money – but they can't eat money either, so they have to use it to buy food from...the big corporations. Junk food at that.

Environmentally friendly

It's not only the workers who are being exploited, though, **Arne Naess** would argue.

Look what the food industry is doing to our environment. Animals are exploited and made to suffer in factory farms, pesticides are killing off meadow creatures and pollinators such as bees, and monoculture is destroying biodiversity. At the same time, excessive consumption of meat and dairy products is creating a demand for grazing land that could be used more productively to grow crops, while the grazing animals produce billions of litres of global-warming methane, and we're creating a climate time bomb shipping all this stuff around the world. We're treating nature as a means to an end, and exploiting it for our own greed.

Maybe Diogenes was right to say that we should live "in harmony with nature", not just for our own good, but for the good of all living things

Making a decision:

If you don't want to think about where your food comes from, you might find an ally in Epicurus on the grounds of convenience and guilty pleasure. Deep down, you might agree with Diogenes of Sinope, however, that convenience food isn't exactly a healthy option, although Geber might provide a counterargument to the idea that natural = good. You might also be swayed by Marx's contention that not questioning how our food is produced is helping the continuation of an unfair capitalist society, or worse, Naess's argument that global agribusiness and the food industry are damaging the planet.

Is Shakespeare better than *The Simpsons?*

Bentham • Mill

We've all had that conversation with friends that starts "Did you see that Shakespeare on the TV last night...?" More often than not, it ends up as a debate on the merits of one show versus another, and inevitably one of the group dismissively saying, "Oh, I don't watch TV." But should you admit that the production of *Hamlet* they're discussing bored you to tears, and you switched channels to catch the one where Homer meets Mick Jagger? And then got a beer and watched the football? Did the Shakespeare buffs really have a better evening than you, or are they just being snobbish?

Plenty of philosophers, from Plato and Aristotle to the present day, have gone to great lengths to explain and justify what they believed constitutes a great work of art. But in a way, they would be missing the point here, because most of the time, they neglect to mention anything about the amount of pleasure people get from them. In fact, a lot of time they seem to be telling us why we should be enjoying them. Anyway, we all know that Shakespeare (and Sophocles, Beethoven, Rembrandt and all the rest) tick all the boxes, but that doesn't mean that we don't get some pleasure out of other things too. A different kind of pleasure, maybe, but pleasure nevertheless.

The thinkers to turn to for advice on this question are the utilitarians, the philosophers who based all their thinking about moral (and aesthetic) decisions on the amount of pleasure or pain that is caused. This school of thought was largely the brainchild of **Jeremy Bentham**, a brilliant and radical English political and social reformer. The first thing he would tell you is that "Nature has placed mankind under the governance of two sovereign masters, pain and pleasure", and that of course you want to minimize one and maximize the other. Pain is bad, pleasure is good. So, to decide whether one thing is "better" than another thing, you need to see whether it gives more pleasure (or at least causes less pain).

Basic philosophical question

Is there a qualitative difference between high culture and popular entertainment?

Whatever turns you on

And you'd need to have some way of measuring that. As it happens, Bentham can give us a handy tool, his *calculus of felicity*. Without going into detail here, this is a sort of points system for weighing up the options, units of pain on one side, and units of pleasure on the other. Now, despite his well-to-do upbringing and fierce intellect, Bentham gave the impression he enjoyed simple pleasures, and had a wicked wit. That he dismissed one argument as "nonsense upon stilts" shows he appreciated fun as much as the cut and thrust of rational debate. And he hated the idea that there is good and bad taste. In the Shakespeare v *Simpsons* case, he would insist that "there is no hierarchy among pleasures" and compare them strictly according to his calculus. In his opinion,

it would be insolent to presume to judge someone's pleasure in a matter of taste.

What's more, he'd point out that the crux of his utilitarian philosophy is "the greatest happiness of the greatest number". Looked at that way, Shakespeare and *The Simpsons* come out pretty much as equals in the long run, but on that criterion you would pretty soon come to the conclusion that the amount of pleasure enjoyed by a football match or a pop festival was way higher than the latest art-house movie or avant-garde concert.

Bentham's godson, **John Stuart Mill**, however, would take a very different view on this subject. Although he admired his godfather enormously, and took up the cause of utilitarianism, he didn't share his mentor's enthusiasm for the calculus of felicity and the "greatest number of people" principle.

> "It is better to be a human being dissatisfied than a pig satisfied; better to be Socrates dissatisfied than a fool satisfied. And if the fool, or the pig, are of a different opinion, it is because they only know their own side of the question"
> John Stuart Mill

Nor did he share Bentham's appreciation of the merits of vulgar pursuits. In fact, he had quite a dig at the old boy, saying that what people get pleasure from tells us a lot about whether they are "wise or a fool, cultivated or ignorant, gentle or rough, sensitive or callous". It's obvious, he said, that some pleasures are "higher" than others, that they are valued more highly and considered more important.

How can you tell which ones they are, though? Mill's answer to that would be to ask people which of two pleasures they enjoyed more, and to make that judgement on quality, not quantity. In the Shakespeare and *Simpsons* example, for instance, he would say that if people had actually experienced both, they might say they had a similar amount of pleasure from both, but would rate the quality of their pleasure in the Shakespeare more highly. In his opinion, we make that judgement because we prefer stimulation of our higher faculties, our intellect and imagination, to simple satisfaction of our baser appetites, our emotions and instincts. But, of course, if they hadn't even seen a Shakespeare play, how could they compare it to *The Simpsons*?

That would explain, he would say, the popularity of many "lower" forms of entertainment, as most people have not had the opportunity to delight in high culture. Instead, they are fed popular culture, sports and games, which merely entertain and amuse. And, like sensual pleasures and satisfaction of physical needs, the enjoyment tends to be ephemeral, while the pleasures of the higher arts better stand the test of time.

Making a decision:

Would you agree with Bentham that the pleasure you get from *The Simpsons* is just as valid as the pleasure others get from Shakespeare? Why should you feel guilty about enjoying things that are not "intellectual" enough? Or do you think Mill is right to make a distinction between activities that satisfy our sensual and instinctive appetites, and art that appeals only to our intellect? And that there's a difference between the pleasure you get from being entertained or amused, and the pleasure you get from appreciating great art?

What's artistic about a pile of junk? Am I missing something?

Plato • Aristotle • Barthes • Dickie

They've got to be joking. If that were outside the gallery, the street-sweeper would scoop it up and take it away. It's not even something a three-year-old would be proud of. How can that be art? It doesn't look like anything other than a pile of junk. Yet there are queues to go and see the damn thing, and no doubt someone will pay a fortune for it. Don't get me wrong – I'm sure they get something from it, but I can't see it myself.

It's nothing new for people to react to art, especially contemporary art, with incomprehension. It's quite possible that in prehistoric times, cave painters came in for criticism of their stylized portrayals of animals and arcane symbols, and we have written records that show the ancient Greeks were sometimes outraged by new styles of sculpture and drama. And no doubt then, as now, there were those who saw themselves as

a cultural elite, and looked down on anybody who was ignorant enough not to appreciate these works of art.

So, when you dismiss that artwork as just a pile of junk, are you pointing out the emperor has no clothes on? Or is it really something with artistic merit? How do you judge the merit of a work or art – and more to the point, what exactly makes something a work of art? That was a hot topic in ancient Greece, and **Plato** had very definite ideas about it. Actually he wasn't too keen on art of any kind, and thought that a decent society would be better off without it. That, he explains, is because art, whether it be painting and sculpture or literature or even music, is artificial. It's an imitation of something in the real world.

A landscape is just a representation of a scene in the natural world. But nature beats it hands down, in Plato's opinion. The same with poetry: just a description, most of the time. And drama – well, that's supposed to represent human life, but let's be honest, it isn't very convincing. All in all, art is nowhere near as inspiring as what it's supposed to represent, it's a sort of corruption of it. And

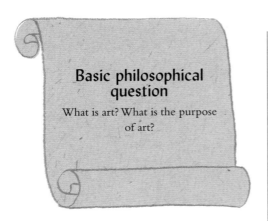

Basic philosophical question

What is art? What is the purpose of art?

that piece you're talking about? Yes, it is a pile of junk, but is that really any worse than carving a lump of rock, or putting some colours on a canvas and saying it represents something? Maybe it's a conceptual artwork, representing an idea rather than a physical object. In that case it's doomed to failure, as it is impossible to match the perfection of something from the world of ideas in a mere representation.

That's an extreme view, and one that not many people would subscribe to, but it does make us think about what art is trying to do, what its purpose is. Which is where Plato's sparring partner **Aristotle** picks up the debate. He too thinks that art is representation, but far from being an imperfect imitation of the natural world or human life, it should be an improvement upon it. At its best, he argues, it is a refinement of the things in the real world, and gives us an insight into its essential qualities. We don't expect art to be a perfect representation, that would be missing the point. A sculptor, for example, will choose to ignore a person's blemishes when creating a statue, and perhaps exaggerate or underplay certain features, to show the character of the subject, or its inherent beauty.

Part of our appreciation of the sculptor's art is admiration of the skill in doing this, but probably the most obvious aspect is our emotional response, Aristotle would explain. It's not a question of how closely the sculptor, artist, playwright or whatever has mimicked real life, but whether a work of art affects us emotionally or intellectually. That's how we judge the worth of art, and even whether something can be considered as a work of art.

You decide

Looking at that pile of junk again, although it doesn't do anything for you, you might concede that other people get aesthetic enjoyment from it, that it arouses some emotion in them or makes them think. Aristotle would say that gives them grounds for regarding it as a work of art, and to the

> "*The aim of art is to represent not the outward appearance of things, but their inward significance*"
> Aristotle

extent that it affects them has artistic merit. **Roland Barthes** (1915–80) would go even further with that argument, saying that it doesn't matter what the artist may have set out to achieve, that's not what determines the significance of a work. It is up to the viewers to actively examine the work and find its meaning for themselves. This is slightly different from simply asking, "Do you like this?" or "Is this beautiful?", or even Aristotle's question of whether it evokes a response from you. Instead, Barthes is saying that the viewer, not the artist, actually creates the significance of a work of art, and even decides whether it is a work of art at all.

From your point of view, it seems Barthes is giving you free rein to reject the pile of junk as just that, if that is the significance you read into it. There are others, however, who would dispute that you are the one to make that judgement. It may even be that we should ignore not only the artist's intentions when judging a work of art, but the viewers' responses too. After all, they are simply subjective, and public taste is very fickle. Just look at what people were calling great art a hundred years ago, and what they were ridiculing as rubbish with no aesthetic or artistic value. So, if it isn't the fact that an artist is creating something

> *"Whatever art is, it is no longer something primarily to be looked at. Stared at, perhaps, but not primarily looked at"*
> Arthur Danto

he or she intends to be a work of art, and it isn't the effect it has on its viewers, what is it that makes it a work of art? And more importantly, who decides?

The artworld

The "artworld", that's who. At least according to **George Dickie** (b. 1926), the champion of the "institutional" theory of art. He would say that something can only be a work of art if it is considered to be a work of art by the institution he calls the artworld. That's not quite as simple, or as simplistic, as it sounds, however. It doesn't mean, for example, that any old pile of junk becomes a work of art simply by being displayed in an art gallery.

To elaborate on his theory, he would explain that terms such as "art", "artist" and "artworld" have very specific meanings, which he defines carefully in setting out the criteria for regarding something as a work of art. The artist, for example, is someone who deliberately creates something, an "artifact", as a work of art. The artifact is then presented to an artworld public, which consists of people who have a knowledge and understanding of art theory and history, and are willing to consider it as a candidate for the status of work of art. If all the artworld public, in other words the artworld in general, agree, then that artifact is a work of art.

You may not like it, but by that definition the pile of junk is officially a work of art, because the artist, and people in the know, say that it is. You're still entitled to your opinion, of course, and it would still be the same pile of junk if the artworld rejected it.

Making a decision

Like many people, you might feel that art should represent something, and be judged on how well it does that. You may even prefer the real thing, as Plato does, to the artistic representation, or agree with Aristotle that art gives us an insight into the world around us. Perhaps you think this pile of junk represents an idea rather than a thing, and as Barthes suggests it's up to the viewer to interpret it, and decide on its artistic merit. Or maybe Dickie is right to say that that should be the job of the experts.

How come that $10 million painting is suddenly worthless now it's been proved a fake?

Plato • Aristotle • Derrida • Searle

The art world is completely crazy. One minute the collectors and galleries are trying to outbid one another to get hold of a painting, and the experts are raving about how wonderful it is, and the next minute it's not worth a red cent. If it was a great picture before, why isn't it now? The only thing that has changed is that somebody has shown that it wasn't painted by the person everybody thought it was painted by. Even if it is a fake, can't you still admire it for what it is, rather than what it claimed to be?

There's a lot at stake here. There will be a few red faces among the experts when an artwork turns out to be a forgery, having been passed off as an undiscovered masterpiece by one of the great painters. And as well as losing someone a large sum of money, it shines a light on the dubious business of equating artistic merit with financial worth. It's surprising, then, that nobody's come up with a simple answer to your question. Or maybe not, as it challenges some of our assumptions about the nature of art and how we value it.

As always, it was the Greek philosophers who kicked off the debate, presenting some very different ideas of what we mean by "art" and what its purpose is. One of the first was **Plato**, whose view of all the arts was based on his theory of how we perceive and understand the world around us. Imagine, he would say, a circle. In your mind, you can picture a perfect circle, but that sort of perfection only exists in the realm of ideas; you could never find such a perfect circle anywhere in the world you live in. All the circles in nature, such as the sun and moon, or the ripples on a pond, have some imperfections. They are just shadows, imperfect imitations of the circle in the world of ideas. Now try to draw a picture of, say, a soap bubble. Even if you're a competent artist, it's likely to be even less perfect than the bubble.

That, Plato would argue, is why he is suspicious of art. It is a crude representation

Basic philosophical question

How do we assess the worth of a work of art? Does a work of art have an intrinsic value, or does it depend on its provenance or context?

Plato's Greengrocer $10

$10m

A bowl of fruit is attractive to look at, as well as good to eat. In contrast, a picture of a bowl of fruit is merely a representation, an imperfect imitation of fruit, and you can't even eat it. So why should it be worth a million times more than the real thing?

of something that itself is a flawed imitation of the perfection that exists only in the realm of ideas. In terms of worth, surely the artwork should be less valued than the thing it is imitating. If you put a $10 million price tag on, for example, a still life with fruit, how much would you say the bowl of fruit is worth? That may seem like a silly question, but can you explain why you would pay more for an imitation than you would for the real thing?

Now, Plato would continue, let's get back to the question of this fake. It's an imitation of a work of art (which itself is a representation of something else), so it is obviously of less quality than what it is

imitating. Plato already has a pretty low opinion of art, so he would naturally value the fake less than the original painting. But using the insane reasoning of the art world, where a representation of an apple is worth more than a whole orchard, perhaps a fake should actually be more highly valued than the original.

An entertaining argument, his friend **Aristotle** would say, but it only works if you accept all that stuff about trying to represent perfect ideas. That, Aristotle says, is not the purpose of art. More than simply represent something, a work of art is created to stimulate our emotions and intellect. So,

> *"Art has no end but its own perfection"*
> Plato

> *"...that a poem or story induces...vivid images, intense feelings, or heightened consciousness, is neither anything which can be refuted nor anything which it is possible for the objective critic to take into account"*
>
> William K. Wimsatt and Monroe Beardsley

we have to look at the fake and see if that does too. If it does, shouldn't we regard it as a work of art, rather than devalue it because it doesn't meet other criteria? Just because the experts have disowned it because of its dubious provenance doesn't mean it can't give us aesthetic pleasure. Nor should we be denied our enjoyment of it because the intention of the artist was to make a fast buck, not a work of art. If even the experts have been fooled by it up to now, it must have artistic merit, and be as aesthetically valuable (or very nearly) as the real thing.

While Aristotle would use that argument to show that it is hypocritical, or just plain snobbish, to put a lower price on a painting because it turns out not to be by a "great master", he would concede that we still feel uncomfortable about discovering something is a fake. Perhaps this is because it not only devalues the artwork, but exposes our response to it as being somehow less than genuine too; the artist didn't set out to arouse our emotions, and we've been fooled into thinking that he did. And for that reason, we feel justified in wiping several million dollars off the asking price.

In context

A completely different slant on the question emerged in the latter part of the 20th century, spearheaded by philosophers such as **Jacques Derrida** (1930–2004). Although his main interest was in literary criticism, he and his fellow post-structuralists proposed a neat solution to the problem of authenticity. They rejected the idea that the author (or in this case, artist) and his or her intentions have any bearing at all on the meaning of a work of art, nor how its merits should be judged. Derrida famously said that "*Il n'y a pas de hors-texte*" (often mistranslated as "There is nothing outside the text", but more accurately, "There is no outside-text" or "There is no out-of-context"), suggesting that, although a work of art must be judged on its merits, context is everything.

So when considering this fake, it's not important who painted the picture or why, but only the context in which it is viewed. We have to look outside the work and its provenance to see what meanings it may have. If the picture is in a gallery with the label "Rembrandt", it has a different context from being in the bin marked fake. And if it is lauded by the critics, this provides a different meaning from its exposure as a forgery by an art historian. None of these sources of context is more nor less valid than any other, and the only consistent thing is the work itself.

The fact that it is a fake may be irrelevant, or the context from which it derives its meaning. For example, it could be interpreted as a conceptual work, its status as a fake being a statement about authenticity, or authority, or the hegemony of artistic norms, or even a critique of the capitalist system that puts an arbitrary monetary value on something intrinsically worthless, and shows that to be hollow when it is discovered to be a fake.

But more probably, it was like the Rolex watches you can buy from street vendors – just a scam. We've been taken for a ride by someone looking for financial gain. So naturally we instinctively feel cheated by the intentions of the forger – which it would appear do turn out to be relevant to how we regard the painting – and this devalues the work in our estimation. As for Derrida's argument to the contrary, perhaps **John Searle** (b. 1932) should have the last word. Like many English-speaking philosophers, he sees Derrida as a pseudo-philosopher,

a fake. And his reasoning is just as much a fake as the painting, an imperfect copy of a philosophical argument. A true philosopher, as Plato explained, can see the difference between the imperfect shadow and the perfect idea.

Making a decision

You might not agree with Plato that all art is an imperfect copy of reality, but he may make you think about why a copy, a fake, should be of less value than an original artwork. Then you might come to the same conclusion as Aristotle: that so long as the fake has the desired effect, it doesn't really matter who painted it or why – an idea endorsed by Derrida. Or maybe, like Searle, you detect the whiff of sophistry in Derrida's arguments.

My favourite singer has been convicted of domestic violence. Do I delete his stuff from my smartphone?

Kant • Schopenhauer • Beardsley • Wimsatt

It's a shock when you find your idols have feet of clay. All your preconceptions about that person are thrown into doubt. And if it's your favourite singer, you probably won't be able to listen to his songs in the same way ever again, with the thought of what he's done at the back of your mind. Maybe it shouldn't affect your judgement of his singing, but it does. In any case, you probably think he doesn't deserve your loyalty any more, but would you be cutting off your nose to spite your face if you got rid of your favourite songs?

When your illusions about someone are shattered, it's difficult to know how to react. Your first instinct is to have nothing to do with that person. But if they have also done something you admire, you're faced with weighing that up against the wrong they've done, and deciding if their sins negate their achievements. Then you have to think about what, if anything, you're going to do about it.

In the case of an artist, such as your singer, there are two aspects to your dilemma: an aesthetic judgement of whether his bad behaviour should affect your attitude to his songs, and the moral problem of whether you effectively turn a blind eye to his crimes by continuing to enjoy his music. The question of morality does seem to be a more serious matter than aesthetic appreciation, so let's deal with that one first. And who better to deal with a serious question than **Immanuel Kant**, whose seriousness is legendary, and whose stance on ethical matters was unequivocal?

He'd ask straight out if you condemn the singer's actions. Which, naturally, you do. Next he'd ask whether, if you had known beforehand that that singer was violent and misogynistic, you would have bought his music. Probably not, because that would implicitly be condoning his behaviour, or at least dismissing it as unimportant. So, Kant would go on, you think it would be morally

Basic philosophical question

Are our artistic judgements of the art or the artist? Can we separate the meaning of a work of art from the intentions of the artist?

141

It's not just overtly sexist or homophobic rap songs you'd have to delete from your playlists, if you're worried about what the artists thought or got up to. Throughout history, great music has been composed or performed by people whose morals were at best questionable. Wagner was an anti-semite, Gesualdo was a murderer, Lewis was allegedly an abusive bigamist, and Glitter was jailed for child sexual abuse.

wrong to buy the music of a convicted wife-beater. And, he would continue, if you think that it is wrong in that case, it is wrong in every case. At the very least, you should not buy any more of his songs, and perhaps you should consider boycotting his music altogether.

Anyway, Kant would add, that singer has been exposed as a thoroughly unpleasant and criminal individual. He's morally corrupt, and that is bound to be reflected in his music, as that is an artistic expression of his character. You might have been unaware of that, until you were shown his true colours, but now you have the opportunity to reappraise his work with that in mind. And then press delete.

Nobody's perfect

Kant's uncompromising ethical standpoint is not everybody's cup of tea, however. Even **Arthur Schopenhauer**, who otherwise idolized Kant, found it difficult to swallow. Probably because his own private life was far from spotless, and no match for Kant's almost monastic existence. As a result, Schopenhauer would advise you to separate your judgement of the person from what you think about his work. Speaking personally, he would tell you that he was frequently accused of saying,

"It is not necessary for a perfectly beautiful person to be a great sculptor, or for a great sculptor to be himself a beautiful person"
Arthur Schopenhauer

> *"The design or intention of the author is neither available nor desirable as a standard for judging the success of a work of [literary] art"*
> William K. Wimsatt and Monroe C. Beardsley

"Do as I say, not as I do", because he didn't live up to the standards of his own moral philosophy. Schopenhauer openly admitted he was no saint, but at the same time in his philosophical writings set out a code of ethics. Just because he found it as difficult as the next man (OK, maybe not Kant) to keep to the straight and narrow, it doesn't mean that his moral philosophy was wrong.

It's the same wherever you look, Schopenhauer would say. Everybody has their flaws. If a politician, for example, is mired in a sex scandal, or is exposed in a video telling some tasteless stories, it shouldn't detract from the trade deal he's just arranged. Of course, if he's shown to be a liar, a tax cheat or simply incompetent, that's a different kettle of fish, as it's directly related to his suitability for the job.

Similarly, we should separate the artist from his art. Beethoven was a self-centred grouch who cheated on his publisher, yet composed the "Ode to Joy"; and Wagner, the composer of the heart-aching opera *Tristan and Isolde*, was a rabid anti-semite. Scratch the surface, and you'll find that many great artists are pretty self-centred and often have pretty murky private lives. Your favourite singer's appalling behaviour doesn't negate what he does on stage or in the studio – but if he were to be found miming to someone else, or ripping off someone else's songs, that would be reason to rethink your attitude to his work.

The art...

Schopenhauer's idea that you should consider the song, not the singer, would be endorsed by **Monroe C. Beardsley** (1915–85), but he would take it a step further. In a sort of double act with literary critic **William K. Wimsatt** (1907–75), Beardsley went the whole hog and proposed that it is a mistake to look to the artist at all when we're making a judgement of a work of art. There's no way, he says, that we can know what an artist had in his mind at the time of creating something, what his feelings, ideas or even intentions were, so we can't use that as a way of interpreting his work. Whatever we might discover about an artist should be irrelevant to making a rational and objective appraisal. Even if these are statements by the artist about his work, or references to it in, for example, letters or diaries, they can be misleading. And accounts of his private life, no matter how accurate or revealing, shouldn't be allowed to cloud our judgement.

... or the artist?

But there's another problem lurking in here, too. Maybe your admiration is for the singer, not the song. You only happen to like the music because it is sung by that particular person, and you are attracted to him perhaps because of his celebrity or the lifestyle and attitudes that are associated with him. No wonder you have been affected so badly by

> "If the world were clear, art would not exist"
> Albert Camus

the revelations. However, this doesn't mean you didn't respond appreciatively to the songs, too. At the time, before the scales fell from your eyes, you were moved by them. And that, Beardsley would say, shows how unreliable an emotional response is when we try to assess the significance of art. There are all sorts of factors that affect the way we feel about a work of art, especially a song. It may have external associations, such as with a fashion or a social group, or it might be forever associated in your mind with the circumstances in which you heard it, especially if they where highly charged emotionally. That may be relevant to you, and the effect the music has upon you, but it is not an intrinsic part of the song itself, so shouldn't be used to support arguments about its artistic merit.

It may, though, be a good enough reason to wipe the songs from your playlist. If your enjoyment of them is influenced by the way you feel about the singer, you won't want to listen to them again. But if you can get past that, and see the music for what it is, then it's a moral decision, not an aesthetic one. Does listening to this singer amount to condoning his behaviour? That's for you to decide.

Making a decision

Your immediate reaction might be to boycott this singer completely, on moral grounds. That would be Kant's position. But Schopenhauer would argue that it's an aesthetic, not a moral decision: the artist's behaviour has nothing to do with it and you can't expect an artist to be a saint. If you agree with that, you would probably also appreciate the arguments of Beardsley and Wimsatt, that we should judge the art and not the artist.

Arthur Schopenhauer

"It is not necessary for a perfectly beautiful person to be a great sculptor, or for a great sculptor to be himself a beautiful person"

Politics

Chapter 5

I'm fed up with people telling me what to think.

Hume • Socrates • Nietzsche • Foucault

Ever since you were a kid, there's been someone telling you how you should behave. Parents, teachers, the local preacher – they've all laid down the law about what is acceptable and unacceptable behaviour, and how to tell the difference between good and bad. You would think that you'd know by now, wouldn't you? But it doesn't stop when you reach adulthood. Every time you turn on the TV, look in the newspaper or even get into a conversation with your friends, somebody gives you the benefit of their superior knowledge and tells you what's right.

Given that you've had enough of being told what you should think, it seems a bit strange that you should be turning to anyone for advice. Yet it does seem that you want something more than just to vent your anger, or maybe to get some affirmation of your feelings; a bit of constructive advice perhaps, rather than a dogmatic opinion? Well, you've come to the right place, then, because although philosophers often have strong opinions, they won't share them unless

Basic philosophical question

Can there be any rational justification for ethical rules? Can we have morality without religion?

they can back them up with arguments. And they'll be more likely to tell you how to think, than what you should think.

Anyway, let's look at your complaint. What you're really saying is that you're fed up with people telling you what they think, and telling you that what you think is wrong. Of course, they can give you their opinion, but you don't have to agree with them. That's fine if they can justify their position with sound, reasoned arguments, and convince you that they're right (or that you're wrong). The problem comes when they start using words such as "must", "should" or "ought to". That's when they cross the line from facts, the stuff of rational argument, to values and opinions. In short, they're telling what they think is good and bad, what is morally right or wrong – and by implication they're telling you what you ought to think, and how you ought to behave.

That, **David Hume** says, is just not on. How can anybody justify moving from an "is" to an "ought"? It's a big leap from explaining how things are to saying how they ought to be, from a descriptive statement to a prescriptive statement. And making that jump is not a rational, logical step, but involves a value judgement rather than facts. You simply can't derive an "ought" from an "is".

Is and ought

Hume would tell you to be careful when anybody is talking about morality or politics, because they'll slip from descriptive to prescriptive statements almost imperceptibly. One minute they'll say that such and such is the case, the next that this ought to be the case. Don't be fooled. Using "Hume's guillotine", the imaginary blade that cuts the world of facts from the world of values, you can see when they're talking sense, or when they're just saying how they'd like things to be.

The sort of things that people are telling you to think, issues of morality or politics, for example, almost always entail that shift from descriptive to prescriptive. And while you can't deny facts, or a sound rational argument, you don't have to accept value judgements. What are they, anyway? Just matters of opinion, and an emotional reaction; in the end, all morality is derived from what Hume calls the "passions", not facts or reason. So when someone says that something ought to be, because it is good, all they are saying is that they approve of it. And implicit in this is the idea "This is good: you should do it" or "This is bad: you shouldn't do it".

Just like a politician giving a speech, they are implicitly looking for confirmation of their opinion. "We should aim for full employment", for example, is just another way of saying, "I think full employment is a good thing", and then expecting a standing ovation. A shorthand version of this would be "Full employment – Hoorah!", or "Unemployment – Boo!", which shows it up as a less than rational way of presenting an argument, no better than saying, "I like

Hume's guillotine

149

One of the arguments in favour of religion is that it provides a moral framework, but atheists would dispute that they are somehow immoral simply because they have no religious belief.

spinach," (Hoorah!) "so should you!"

The people trying to convince you of their ideas of morality would dispute that, of course. Notions of good and bad, right and wrong, aren't just matters of opinion but come with some sort of authority. Religion, for example, is a source of many of the "shoulds" and "should nots", and you can't get a much higher authority than God. It's often argued that religion is necessary, because without it there would be no morality.

But **Socrates** dared to challenge that idea, not by saying it was wrong, but in his usual way by questioning the premise of the argument: the gods love what is good. Are the good things good because the gods love them, then? Or do the gods love them because they're good? In other words, do the gods determine what is good? If they do, then by doing good we're just blindly obeying arbitrary rules whose only justification is the approval of the gods, and the gods could be commanding us to do all sorts of dubious things. But if the gods love things because they're good, then those things are good independently of the gods – so we could discover what is good without referring to the gods.

If the gods' authority is questionable on questions of morality, then so is the authority of the priests. And teachers, and politicians...

and in fact anybody who is telling you what you should think. If they're telling you to do or think something because it's right, they're irrelevant to its rightness, and you could work that out for yourself. And if it's only right because they say it is, it would be a mistake to follow them blindly without some better evidence. Either way, Socrates is suggesting very strongly that it's better to come to your own conclusions about what's morally right or wrong.

Slaves and masters

That's very much the conclusion **Friedrich Nietzsche** came to. He was brought up in a very religious family, to the strict moral standards imposed by his father's Lutheran protestantism. When he had a crisis of faith as a young man, and realized that "God is dead", he recognized that nearly all our ideas of morality come from religion, and without it we are free to make our own ethical code.

Unfortunately, the majority of people can't get away from the ethics they've been brought up with, and the annoying habit of preaching the same old misguided nonsense about good and evil. Even in secular societies, the pervasive influence of religious morals lingers on, and by instilling fear and guilt into everybody stops them from discovering for themselves what is right and wrong.

Worse than that, though, Nietzsche would add, the morals that are being foisted on us by religion, and these days governments too, don't come from God, but from the religious leaders. And they were designed to keep ordinary people like you in their place. By telling you that qualities such as meekness, pacifism and even poverty are "good" (Hoorah!), the leaders of society retain control of a submissive populace. Meanwhile, the suckers who swallow that line, what Nietzsche refers to as "slave morality", keep turning the other cheek and perpetuating the myths. So long as this persists, Nietzsche would say, there will always be people who will tell you what to think, and how to behave, but you can choose not to listen and follow your own path.

It's not that simple, however, according to **Michel Foucault**. It's not just a ruling class imposing a system of ethics on us in order to hold on to power. It's subtler and more insidious than that. OK, it's true that authority figures, such as parents, teachers, religious leaders and politicians can enforce their moral codes on us by a system of punishments and rewards in order to exert their power, but who is pulling their strings? And anyway, do we just behave the way we do out of fear, or in the hope that we will be rewarded?

"Morality is herd instinct in the individual"
Friedrich Nietzsche

No, Foucault says, power is being exercised everywhere in society, not just by rulers over their subjects. Instead of real morality, we have cultural and societal norms that are constantly being reinforced by the way everybody in society behaves. We don't have to be explicitly told what to think, because we're constantly being shown what is and isn't acceptable.

Once a particular behaviour or idea becomes the norm, by implication it must be a "good" thing, and any deviation from that norm is wrong. You don't have to be told what to think, because any "deviant" thinking is taboo, and literally unthinkable. Rulers, even in repressive regimes, aren't so much imposing their ideas on others, as being given that power by the prevailing standards of morality; they are symptoms rather than causes. Although they might say, for example, that homosexuality is a punishable offence, this is only a reflection of that society's taboos, and for most of its citizens it would be impossible to imagine otherwise. And because it's so deeply ingrained in the thinking of that society, it's difficult not to be persuaded to think the same – without any obvious pressure being put on you.

If you believe you're constantly being told what to think, Foucault would say, lucky for you! Most people don't even know how their thoughts and actions are being manipulated, let alone who is really controlling the agenda. So don't get mad, get active. You've obviously got a mind of your own, so use it to challenge the ubiquitous power of received wisdom.

Making a decision

If you're wary of people who tell you what you should do, say or think, you'd find a staunch ally in Hume. It's one thing, he says, to say how things are, and quite another to say how they should be. Socrates could also provide ammunition for attacking the people who rely on religious authority to tell you how to think. And if you want support for the idea that you can decide for yourself what to think, you need look no further than Nietzsche and Foucault.

Why can't I decide who to vote for?

Plato • Aristotle • Hobbes

It's election time again, and you are bombarded with information about the candidates standing, and the parties they represent. How do you choose which one is best for the job? Each one of them has more or less convincing arguments about their policies – how they'll run the economy, defend the country and look after our well-being. You want someone who'll run the country properly, or at least protect your interests. But politicians are all the same, aren't they? They'll promise anything to get elected, and then just look after themselves and their cronies…

Most countries in the world today are, to a greater or lesser extent, democratic. That is, the majority of adults have a say in who governs them, and voting in elections is generally recognized as a fundamental human right. It has not always been like that, though, and the right to vote has often been hard fought for. Choosing who to give your vote to is quite a responsibility, then, but often not an easy decision to make.

The roots of western democracy lie in classical Athens, when a tyrannical ruler was overthrown in 510 BCE, and the people of the city decided, unusually, to choose how they should be governed. **Plato** saw this as an opportunity to organize society along rational lines, rather than let it be dictated by some hereditary ruler or whoever had the strongest army, and set out his ideas in *The Republic*. While he was happy to be rid of tyranny, he wasn't really a fan of democracy. In his opinion, government should be to enable the citizens to live a "good life". But the only people who understand the

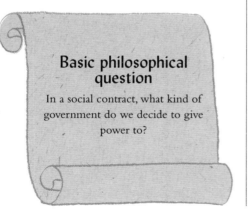

Basic philosophical question

In a social contract, what kind of government do we decide to give power to?

"The office of the sovereign, be it a monarch or an assembly, consisteth in the end for which he was trusted with the sovereign power, namely the procuration of the safety of the people"
Thomas Hobbes

The political spectrum and where political thinkers lie on it

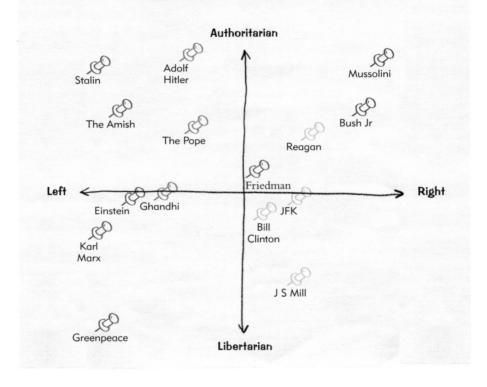

Authoritarian

Stalin   Adolf Hitler   Mussolini

The Amish   The Pope   Bush Jr

Reagan

Left ← Friedman → **Right**

Einstein   Ghandhi   JFK

Karl Marx   Bill Clinton

J S Mill

Greenpeace   **Libertarian**

---

moral values necessary for that good life are philosophers like himself. So, government should be by a ruling class of "philosopher-kings". Arrogant, certainly, but perhaps he had a point: in deciding who to vote for, you should consider which candidates have the necessary knowledge and skills to do the job.

Cui bono?

Aristotle, on the other hand, asked two simple questions: who rules? And in whose interests? A good government is one that rules in the interests of the state as a whole, while one that rules in the interest of those in power is what he called corrupt. Then, he applied these criteria to three different types of rule in order to compare them: an individual ruler (either a good monarch or a tyrannical dictator), a small ruling class (a benign aristocracy or a corrupt oligarchy) or the people – who could rule either for the common good in constitutional government,

VOTE PLATO

A safe pair of hands

VOTE HOBBES

For law and order

VOTE ARISTOTLE

To make your voice heard

VOTE ROUSSEAU

Power to the people!

or in their own interests in a democracy. The question "in whose interests" is a shrewd one, and may help you to make up your mind, not only about a candidate's motives for seeking office, but also about whether you're voting for what's best for society or for yourself personally.

The question remains, though, as to what government is actually for. The Greeks were a bit theoretical about this, talking about moral values and the like. It took an Englishman, **Thomas Hobbes**, to be blunt enough to say what things would be like without some kind of rule. In a state of nature, he explained, human life would be "solitary, poore, nasty, brutish, and short", with everyone battling with everyone else for what they wanted. Rather than this sorry state of affairs, we have created a "social contract" between the people and the government, giving up some of our freedoms in return for the protection of the state.

> *"What man loses by the social contract is his natural liberty and an unlimited right to everything he tries to get and succeeds in getting; what he gains is civil liberty and the proprietorship of all he possesses"*
>
> Jean-Jacques Rousseau

Hobbes was all in favour of an authoritarian sovereign, to prevent the kind of anarchy he described so vividly, but others, such as **Jean-Jacques Rousseau**, saw the social contract as a kind of necessary evil, an infringement of our natural liberty. He wanted to give sovereignty to the people, so that government could be administered by the "general will", rather than imposed upon us. From these different views of the relationship between government and people evolved a whole spectrum of political opinion, especially concerning how much government should control our social and economic freedoms. It is up to you to decide where you stand on that spectrum when choosing which candidate gets your vote. Do you vote for a libertarian or an authoritarian? Or, put another way, do you want more personal freedom, or are you prepared to give up some liberties for a more orderly society? And do you vote for the capitalist- or socialist-leaning candidate? Is economic freedom more important than equality? Which is better for you personally – and which is better for society?

Making a decision

You're choosing who should govern as well as who should represent you. So, you might agree with Plato that that person ought to be the one with the best knowledge of how to do that. But you'd also like to know in whose interests he or she is acting, using Aristotle's criteria. Would it be best to go with Hobbes's suggestion of an authoritarian ruler, or Rousseau's democratic dream of a society governed by the will of the people?

"Until philosophers are kings, or the kings and princes of this world have the spirit and power of philosophy... cities will never have rest from their evils."

Plato

Why do politicians never give a straight answer?

Kant • Machiavelli • Socrates • Hume

If you ask a politician the time, he'll tell you about the problems in the clock-making industry. And probably that his opponent's watch is always slow. Occasionally you'll find one who does answer the question, and you find out later she was being "economical with the truth". TV interviews and debates are just like game shows now, the winner being the one who can evade the most. It doesn't exactly inspire confidence in the people who ask us to trust them to run the country. So why do they do that?

We've got a real philosophical conundrum here, because asking philosophers that question is unlikely to get a straight answer either. And, like politicians, philosophers are going to give you some widely differing opinions on the subject. But as you've asked... Probably the most forthright answer you're going to get is from **Immanuel Kant**. Which is surprising, really, given his often impenetrable style of explaining things. But for once he'd come right out and condemn the politicians who don't tell it like it is. In his book, there's no justification for not telling the truth, always. And that means that it's wrong not just to tell an outright lie, but also to try to pull the wool over the voters' eyes. Which is what most politicians do: they blind voters with dubious facts and figures, or avoid the question by giving an irrelevant reply to a completely different question.

Their reasons for doing that don't come into it. They all profess to be telling you the truth – and often accuse their opponents of not being straight – so they have a duty to tell you no more nor less than the truth. We

have a right to expect that of them, so that we can make informed decisions about them, their policies and their fitness to govern. And if they can't do that, don't give them your vote. They can't be trusted.

Need to know

As you might expect, however, that's not how **Niccolò Machiavelli** sees things. As well as being a philosopher, he worked as a diplomat and political advisor, so takes a more practical approach, very much from the politician's perspective. He'd tell you that all that political bluster and evasion is very deliberate. It's what he'd advise a politician to do. Why? Because there are so many things a politician needs to keep from the public. Being cynical (which is something Machiavelli is pretty good at), it could be to cover up for the politician's incompetence, ignorance of the facts of the matter or that the situation is worse than he'd like you to believe.

But there are nobler motives, too. Even a basically good politician will have trouble getting the electorate onside, especially if

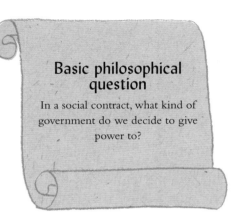

Basic philosophical question

In a social contract, what kind of government do we decide to give power to?

she's got to make some tough decisions. If she told them the straight truth they'd be horrified, and she'd never be given the power to do what is necessary. The people don't need to know, they need to be wooed, and reassured. She also has to be careful not to be too specific, and above all make no promises, as she might be proved wrong and appear incompetent, or worse still be branded as a liar. Then nobody would believe her again. That's why politicians hedge their bets whenever they can. It gives them room for later changes of heart and evolving circumstances.

If pressed, Machiavelli might be persuaded to give some advice to the voter. Bear in mind his advice to politicians, and give them the benefit of the doubt if they seem to be

prevaricating. And beware of the one who prides himself on being a straight talker, in contrast to his equivocating opponent. He may well be just giving you what you want to hear, and if not an outright lie, not the whole truth.

That's similar to the way **Socrates** would regard the dogmatic politician. In general, Socrates had no time for politicians, but not because they don't give straight answers – quite the opposite. Too often, in his opinion, politicians give their opinions as if they were incontrovertible truths, when they should be trying to get to the nub of the question. And while a bad politician will use an evasive answer to hide his ignorance, the best, in his opinion, will openly admit he doesn't have all the answers. By using Socrates's method of challenging any claims and countering leading questions with yet more questions, this sort of politician is not avoiding an answer. Far from it. He's exposing the inconsistencies and contradictions in his opponent's (or interviewer's) arguments, and attempting to get at the truth. There's a snag, of course. Constantly answering a question with a question, and picking holes in the opposition isn't going to win you any popularity, as Socrates found to his cost. The voters want answers, not more questions, and to be told the truth, plain and simple.

"By a lie a man throws away and, as it were, annihilates his dignity as a man"
Immanuel Kant

> *"A wise man…proportions his belief to the evidence"*
> David Hume

The trouble is, the truth is not always plain and simple. It's not quite as black and white as that, **David Hume** would argue. And although Hume doesn't exactly leap to the defence of shifty politicians, he does explain why they might seem to be less than straightforward. There are, he explains, different kinds of truth. Some statements are unarguably true; they're what he calls "demonstrative statements". The classic example is a statement such as 2 + 2 = 4. That's self-evidently true, and we can see that it's true just by thinking about it. It would be a logical contradiction to say that 2+ 2 does not equal 4, so it must be true. If only politics were that simple.

Which of course it isn't, and Hume would go on to explain why. As well as demonstrative statements, there are, he says, what he calls "probable statements", statements we can't tell are true or false just by thinking about them. We have to look to the real world to see if there is any evidence. If your friend says, for example, that he has $2 in his pocket, you don't know if that is true or false without looking at the contents of his pocket. Whereas a demonstrative statement such as 2 + 2 = 4 is a matter of reasoning, the probable statement that your friend has $2 in his pocket is a matter of fact. To make that a bit clearer, Hume would explain that the truth of the statement 2 + 2 = 4 is a "necessary truth", it can't be contradicted; but it is possible to deny the truth of the statement that your friend has $2 in his pocket without any logical

Getting at the truth

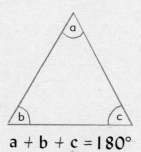

$$a + b + c = 180°$$

$10

The truth that the angles of a triangle add up to a total of 180° is a truth of reasoning – we can see that it is true by thinking about it. But the statement that I have $10 in my piggy bank can only be verified by looking inside the piggy bank and counting the cash; it is a contingent truth, which we have to check

My policies, of course, are contingent on the facts...

Politics is all about contingent truths, and so the statements politicians make are invariably what Hume would call probable statements, dependent for their truth on the evidence we have for them, the facts. And although some statements can be convincingly verified, such as that the national debt is now $X million, there are many more grey areas, such as claims that the debt can be paid off within five years. With probable statements, it's not even a simple matter of true or false, but a degree of probability that can only be determined by the strength of the evidence available to support it.

No wonder, then, that politicians avoid committing themselves. In the final analysis, on balance and taking into account the facts as we know them, it is probable that politicians don't give straight answers for much the same reason as philosophers don't give straight answers: no matter how simple you might think the questions are, there are seldom any simple answers.

contradiction, because it is a "contingent truth", dependent on what actually happens to be the case, the facts.

No simple answers

The problem is that there are very few necessary truths, truths of reasoning, outside the abstract world of mathematics and logic.

Making a decision

You are probably in accord with Kant on this, and think that politicians should always tell the truth, the whole truth and nothing but the truth. But you might like to consider Machiavelli's more pragmatic approach, that politicians are not always trying to cover up their inadequacies, and may have the country's interests at heart, or Socrates's argument that they may also be trying to get at the truth, rather than evading an answer. And you may perhaps agree with Hume that the truth is a rather elusive concept.

I'm trying to run a business, but the regulations, bureaucracy and taxes are making it almost impossible.

Smith • Hume • Marx

It's a wonder anything gets done these days. The people producing the goods, creating the wealth and providing jobs are being hampered all the way by government interference. It's a nightmare trying to keep up with all the rules, and we spend more time dealing with the red tape than getting on with the job. And it costs a fortune, complying with health and safety regulations, consumer protection laws and paying a minimum wage. For what? A great chunk of the profit we make is swallowed up in taxes. Give us a break.

It sounds very much like you're hankering after the good old days, when entrepreneurs were free to get on with what they do best, producing the goods and making money, and governments kept their noses out of business. But did such a golden age ever actually exist? Given that modern industry and the capitalist market economy evolved some time after our modern systems of government had been established, this scenario seems unlikely. No matter how libertarian a government professes to be, its *raison d'être* is to legislate, and it's therefore bound to want to exercise some control over businesses for the good of the country.

Whether that's a good thing or a bad thing is up for debate. The generally accepted authority on this subject is **Adam Smith** who, while not exactly the architect of the market economy, was one of the first to analyse how it works, and recognize its strengths and weaknesses. And he, you might be relieved to hear, would put up a very good case for leaving businesses alone. It's competition in free markets that drives productivity, Smith says, and determines prices. It's a question of supply and demand, and in the long term, the two will balance out so that consumers get the goods they want at a fair price, and producers sell their

> *"Whenever the legislature attempts to regulate the differences between masters and their workmen, its counsellors are always the masters"*
> Adam Smith

> *"It is, therefore, a just political maxim, that*
> *every man must be supposed a knave"*
> David Hume

goods for a fair profit. No government intervention is necessary, or desirable.

Or at least, little government intervention, Smith would say. In an ideal world, businesses could be trusted to produce their goods ethically, and treat their customers fairly, but alas we live in an imperfect world. It's a shame, Smith admits, but there have to be some laws to stop unscrupulous traders. Not really regulation of the market itself, but just to make sure it's working as it should. For example, if only one business is producing a particular product, then there's no competition and the consumer is at that company's mercy, forced to pay any price it cares to name. So you have to have a law preventing monopolies. Then, of course, you have to stop businesses from colluding to form cartels to fix prices and control

supply of goods in the same way. And it goes without saying that there must be laws against insider trading, fraud, cheating and so on. Not to mention some legislation about selling faulty or dangerous goods.

An imperfect system

Smith would concede that the system isn't perfect, and having that sort of regulation is sadly necessary because there will always be people who find the loopholes and exploit them. He would also admit that giving businesses a completely free hand not only skews the consumer–supplier relationship, but can lead to exploitation of the workforce. Smith was all too aware of the evils of slave labour and child labour, and the working conditions of many people who were

earning a pittance, so would not have any objections to government intervention to ameliorate their situation.

The thing is, he would say, that although there has to be some government intervention, this should be to allow businesses to operate fairly in the market system, and should not be so restrictive that it discourages enterprise and innovation. Governments can help to protect people from unscrupulous businesses, but in the main they should stick to looking after the interests of the state and its citizens.

It's at this point that Smith's friend **David Hume** might usefully join the discussion. He would broadly agree with Smith's defence of a business's right to look after its own affairs, but would point out that there are some things the market economy is not equipped to provide. Street lights, for example. No sensible entrepreneur would try to sell them on the open market, because who would buy something that everybody else can then use free of charge? They're public goods, and so should be paid for out of the public purse. And that's the government's responsibility, but to raise the money they have to impose taxes. The same goes for things like the armed forces and the police: they're there to defend and protect everybody, so we should all contribute to paying for them. There's

> ### Basic philosophical question
> How much does a government have the right to intervene in private business? Does government have a duty to protect consumers and employees? Should industry be publicly owned and run?

even a good case to be made for funding other parts of the country's infrastructure, such as roads and railways, electricity and water supplies, and even education, healthcare and welfare payments. And as businesses will benefit as much as anybody from these things, they should pay a share of those taxes too. Unfortunately, that does mean that governments have to exercise some power over businesses, which could be seen as interfering with their ability to make a profit.

Quite right, Smith would reply. The principle of free enterprise still stands, of course, but doesn't work perfectly in practice. So, there has to be some regulation, and some charges have to be made. It's a pity, though, Hume would continue, that the

> *"The process is so complicated that it offers ever so many occasions for running abnormally"*
> Karl Marx

regulation has to be so restrictive. Because it has to deal with all the shortcomings of the market system, and especially to foresee every trick in the book, the law tends to treat everybody as if they're trying to get away with something, and can end up being a sledgehammer to crack a nut. Ironically, that means the small businesses often get hit hardest, tied up with red tape and burdened with high taxes, while the big corporations have the resources to find ways of getting round the laws and avoiding their taxes.

State control

According to Smith and Hume, then, if you want to run a business, you're going to have to put up with some outside interference. But for **Karl Marx**, the situation you're describing is a symptom of a terminal disease. Like Smith, Marx devoted a lot of time and thought to analysing the workings of the market economy, but although he too admired the way it encouraged innovation and created wealth, he questioned the validity of the system. He would argue that for a system that prides itself on thriving without freedom, it needs a heck of a lot of intervention to make it work at all, let alone fairly. Rather than continually tinkering with it to keep it going, why not go the whole hog and have the government making all the rules? Bring all business into state control, let the people own the means of production, and then there would be no need to legislate against unfair business practices and exploitation. You wouldn't need to worry about running a competitive business at all, but instead devote your energies to producing the goods and services that will benefit society as a whole.

Making a decision

From your perspective as an entrepreneur, bureaucracy is not only restrictive, but unnecessary. And Smith would, to a large extent, back you up in that assertion, arguing that regulation is a hindrance to the free market. But perhaps you would concede, as he does, that there are some instances where the market needs some assistance, and even agree with Hume that for the public good there has to be some government intervention. You may even be persuaded by Marx to go the whole hog and accept that capitalism is fundamentally flawed, and that society as a whole should benefit from industry and commerce: they should be in the hands of the people.

Should I trust the predictions of the so-called "experts"?

Confucius • Machiavelli • Hume

According to some politicians, if we don't follow their policies, the country's going to end up even broker than it is now. But their opponents point to evidence that shows just the opposite. Economists are forever telling us they can predict the effects of different policies on the markets. They didn't see the global financial crash coming, though, did they? And now just about every scientist says our fossil-fuel habit is causing climate change, but some politicians and economists maintain they've got it wrong. Who are we supposed to believe?

The sad truth is that politicians are among the least trusted people in society, after real-estate agents and salesmen. And they know it. So, to convince the electorate of the validity of their claims and promises, they cite the evidence of experts – economists, scientists, academics and business people (but not, interestingly, philosophers). More often than not, these experts are quoted to endorse the politicians' claims of how their policies will be best for the voters, or how their opponents' policies will lead to ruin.

The experts are therefore in the business of predicting the future. The trouble is that prediction has a reputation of unreliability. And maybe unfairly so; the weather forecaster may get it right 364 days of the year, but the time she didn't spot the hurricane coming is the one people remember, and she is trusted about as much as the horoscope. Mud sticks, and we're instinctively suspicious of expert forecasts, almost as much as we are of political promises.

As we ought to be, **Confucius** would say. If we need to know whether somebody's claims can be trusted, we should look not at the evidence that is being cited, but at the person making the claim. The "superior man", the person you can put your trust in, Confucius tells us, leads by example, not by making claims and promises. Whether

Basic philosophical question

Can the future ever be predicted with certainty? Is there any rational justification for believing that one thing causes another?

it's politicians, experts or anybody else, they should be judged on their records, what they have done rather than what they say, to see if they are trustworthy. Only then can we examine their predictions.

Even then, you should continue to be on the lookout for signs that the claim is made by an "inferior man", someone who has his own interests at heart. A politician might cite, for example, expert evidence that cannabis can be used to treat cancer, and that he would legalize it. If true, that would be wonderful, but does he have an ulterior motive for saying that? Is he courting popularity, telling the millions of cannabis users what they want to hear? Or maybe his expert advisor tells him that chocolate is the miracle cure. If the politician is sponsored by a confectionery corporation, who funded the research, that person is unlikely to be "superior".

Get real

It's all very well being so noble, **Niccolò Machiavelli** would tell Confucius, but the worlds of politics, diplomacy and business don't work like that. Confucius got it sort of half right, in that we should look at the person, not the claims and predictions. But that's because we all know that you can't trust what they say anyway – they all tell us what they think we want to hear to get our support. And that may not be a bad thing, Machiavelli would argue. A successful politician may be demonstrating skills of persuasion that could be of benefit to his constituents too. The world of politics and diplomacy isn't as gentlemanly and clear-cut as you might like it to be, and somebody who is a bit devious but on your side might be an asset. Besides, he probably understands the situation better than his electorate, but in order to do anything, needs to be put into a position of power or authority – and will promise a rosy future based on the predictions of experts to get there. The point is not whether we trust the predictions and promises, but whether we trust the person to do the job.

David Hume, however, would ask us to look at the whole business of prediction from a different angle. Although he is famously sceptical about most things, not least the motives politicians might have for their

> *"The superior man understands what is right; the inferior man understands what will sell"*
> Confucius

> *"Cunning and deceit will every time serve a man better than force to rise from a base condition to great fortune"*
> Niccolò Machiavelli

claims and promises, he has some sympathy for forecasters. Not that he lets them off the hook completely, because he doubts the validity of any kind of prediction.

One of the problems, he explains, is that we tend to expect certain things to happen, without any rational reason for thinking that they will. If every time we do something, such as eating a certain kind of mushroom, it is followed by our being violently sick, we soon come to the conclusion that the mushroom is causing our illness. And because we've become accustomed to the idea that every time we eat that mushroom we are sick, we predict that if we eat it in the future, we'll be sick again.

That would seem to be just common sense, Hume agrees, but it isn't rational. Just because every time A happens, B follows, we can't assume that A causes B. Let's take a different example. You're a heavy sleeper, and so have two alarm clocks. One tells the correct time, the other is a couple of minutes slow. Every morning, the first clock goes off, and shortly afterward the second one goes off. Every time. Does your "common sense" tell you that the first alarm caused the other clock to go off? Of course not.

The only evidence that the mushrooms cause sickness is what Hume calls a "constant conjunction" of the two events. But as we've seen from the alarm clocks, that's not a good enough basis for jumping to that conclusion. Nevertheless, that's what we do, and most of the time our predictions based on the idea that one thing causes another turn out to

Two alarm clocks are set to go off at 7 o'clock. Clock A duly rings at 7. But clock B has not been synchronized with clock A, and rings a little later. This, of course, happens every morning. First clock A rings, then clock B rings. Does A cause B to ring?

> *"Custom, then, is the great guide of human life"*
> David Hume

be right. So when a scientist tells you that carbon emissions cause global warming, and there will be disastrous climate change if we don't stop burning fossil fuels, we'd be inclined to believe her.

It's a question of basing our predictions on the evidence of our experience, to a large extent. The more often that we see event B following event A, the more likely we are to think that B is caused by A. Every time I get near a cat, I sneeze: so, cats cause me to sneeze. But if it's a one-off, there's not much evidence for causality. For instance, a left-wing government was elected in Ruritania, and the very next day there was a global financial crisis. You'd be hard pushed to argue that the Ruritanian election caused the crash, because there isn't that "constant conjunction". And predictions often depend on the argument that X will happen, because it is caused by Y. So when Y happens, then it

will be followed by X. A sound argument, so long as you accept the premise that Y really does cause X. And the only reason we've got for believing that is that's what has always happened. As far as we know. Of course, there may be instances where it didn't turn out that way, but we just don't know about them.

Now if that sounds a bit evasive, Hume would apologise, it's because he is torn between common sense and rational thinking himself. We like to think, and common sense tells us, that we can get a good idea of what's likely to happen by looking at past experience (what Hume calls "custom"), but we need to examine the evidence carefully, and temper our gut reaction to any prediction with a rational appraisal of how probable it is. And remember that experts sometimes get it hopelessly wrong because they are doing exactly the same.

Making a decision

Do we have a right to expect our politicians and their advisors to have integrity? It's likely that you go along with Confucius in saying yes to that, and look to their records to see who might have ulterior motives. If you're a bit more cynical, you might agree with Machiavelli that politics and diplomacy are "dark arts", and we should go with the people who get the job done. Or maybe you look on the experts more kindly, as Hume does, and accept that prediction can never be an exact science, and we have to rely on our common sense.

I'm as mad as hell with this government. What can I do to make them listen to me?

Marx • Voltaire • Thoreau • Rousseau

Democracy? You're kidding. Once every few years, you get to make your mark on a ballot paper, and that's it. The rest of the time, governments are left to their own devices and do all sorts of unfair, dangerous and downright mad things, and you're reduced to shouting at the TV and radio, or choking on your breakfast as you read the newspaper. They're making decisions that affect the lives of millions, starting wars, destroying the environment, wasting public money...and you're powerless to do anything about it. Or are you?

There's no shortage of philosophers who would tell you that it's healthy to dissent. In fact, pretty much all of them have challenged received wisdom and authority at one time or another. And some of them (Socrates, for example; *see* page 113) ended up paying the price for getting on the wrong side of the powers that be. Not so many, though, have anything useful to say about how you should go about making your voice heard, or actually getting anything done. As **Karl Marx** said, "Philosophers have only interpreted the world, in various ways. The point, however, is to change it." We'll get back to him in a minute.

Let's start, however, with someone who was continually in hot water for speaking his mind, and was a fierce advocate of the right to free speech: **Voltaire** (1694–1778). Though he never actually said it, his view on the matter was that, although he might disagree with what you say, he would defend to the death your right to say it.

That doesn't mean that he'd advise you to carry on moaning at the news, though. It might help you to let off steam, but it's an empty gesture. No, Voltaire was a passionate believer in the power of words, and especially the written word, to bring about change. Instead of directing your rants at the TV, channel those thoughts into letters to the paper, writing books and articles, starting a blog and publishing your views for all to

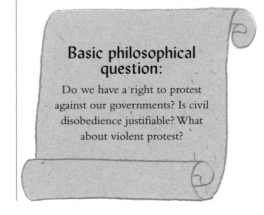

Basic philosophical question:

Do we have a right to protest against our governments? Is civil disobedience justifiable? What about violent protest?

see. Campaign for a free press, with proper investigative journalists, who will expose the shortcomings and corruption of the authorities. It will annoy the hell out of them – much more satisfying than just venting – and may well gain momentum, snowball into a protest movement, influence public opinion and bring about reform.

Civil disobedience

We're not all as extrovert as Voltaire, though, or so witty with words. Not to worry, says **Henry David Thoreau**, you can still get their attention. He'd tell you how, from his cabin in New England, far from the corridors of power, he made headline news, prompting public debate and putting the

government on the back foot. By doing nothing. Or at least, not doing something. He simply didn't pay the taxes he thought were being immorally used to finance the war in Mexico. He would argue that that act of civil disobedience may have been breaking the law of the land (and getting a good bit of publicity into the bargain), but he was following a moral law that trumped it. Laws are made by governments, and they're not always good. In fact, Thoreau would say, a lot of them are bad and contradict the moral code of decent human beings. In such cases, not only is it permissible to break the law, it is your moral duty to do so, and not "resign one's conscience to the legislator". It's no good telling governments that you don't

> *"It is dangerous to be right in matters on which the established authorities are wrong"*
> Voltaire

agree with what they're doing, you have to show them (and the public) what you think of their laws, and expose their injustice and immorality. Without breaking your own moral code, you can use a symbolic violation of the law to make a nuisance of yourself. It could be a simple refusal to pay a tax, or a more serious conscientious objection to a call-up to the forces. Rosa Parks triggered a whole civil rights movement by just sitting in a forbidden seat on a bus. Non-cooperation is good, too – look at what Gandhi achieved just by being awkward.

Direct action

If Thoreau has whetted your appetite for protest, you might like to consider a more active form of resistance. Again, following Thoreau's dictum of not compromising your own principles, this would have to be a minor infringement of the law, but instead of simply not complying, you could indulge in a bit of direct action. Obstruction, maybe, such as taking up residence in a tree-house to prevent the bulldozers flattening woodland. Or a gestural destruction of property, such as cutting a wire in the fence of a military base.

Hold on, you say, aren't we straying a bit far from Thoreau's quiet non-compliance? He would probably agree that those aren't the methods he himself would choose, but applaud the sentiment of challenging bad laws. When it comes to active protest, you would do better to turn to someone else for practical tips.

Which brings us back to Marx. He was a contemporary of Thoreau, and shared his disdain for bad laws and bad government, but had a particular contempt for what he saw as the immorality of capitalism. And, as mentioned earlier, he wasn't content just to voice his opinions, but believed that it is our responsibility to change things. While Thoreau was a scholarly introvert, Marx was a fiery street fighter, and didn't suffer fools gladly. If you're really as mad as hell with the government, he's probably the philosopher you'd most want as your advisor.

Marx had formed his views in the turbulent early 19th century, only a short while after the French and American Revolutions had really shown their governments what they thought of them. And Marx agreed with **Jean-Jacques Rousseau** (a contemporary of that other French firebrand, Voltaire) that government, and in fact the whole system, favours the haves over the have-nots. Instead of giving us freedom, so-called civil society has put ordinary working people in chains, making it almost impossible to bring about reform.

Luckily for you, Marx would tell you, he has a few strategies up his sleeve. That Thoreau, his heart's in the right place, but one individual not paying tax is hardly likely to bring a government to its knees, is it? There has to be a mass movement, and that means informing and educating the people, raising their consciousness of the situation they're in. Yes, like Voltaire said, write

> *"There is only one way in which the murderous death agonies of the old society and the bloody birth throes of the new society can be shortened, simplified and concentrated, and that way is revolutionary terror"*
> Karl Marx

pamphlets, posters and blogs, but not directed at the government: aim for the people, and get them as angry as you are. Once you've reached critical mass, you can start organizing protests. As long as you've got enough people with you, demonstrations, marches, petitions and even occupation of official buildings can be effective. And don't forget the power of the workers. It's not called a workforce for nothing. United, the workers can break free of their chains, bringing economic pressure to bear on their employers and the government.

Seizing power

The problem, Marx would have to concede, is that governments don't always fight fair, and would probably resort to violent tactics to quell that sort of protest. So, we would have to look at the bigger picture, and maybe adopt a more Machiavellian approach ourselves – the ends justify the means. After all, even Thoreau said that it is a moral duty to break the law if it's a bad law.

Those in power will obviously not give it up willingly, so power has to be taken from them, violently if necessary. Because the people's voice has been suppressed, their struggle for change, the class struggle, has become a just war. If you're not prepared to accept some violent protest, you're going to go on impotently shaking your fist at the TV and shouting at the radio.

Making a decision:

Rather than just complaining, you want your voice to be heard, and your opinion to count for something. You could follow Voltaire's advice and make sure your views are publicized, and support the freedom of the press. Or you might want to go a bit further, like Thoreau, and register your disapproval by a bit of constructive objection and civil disobedience, or even some non-violent direct action. And if you're really opposed to what your government is up to, you might consider Rousseau and Marx's advocacy of a revolution to overthrow it.

These days, I'm afraid to go out of my own front door.

Hobbes • Locke • Mill • Camus • Foucault

You just have to look at the headlines. Crime is on the up, and we're living in constant fear of terrorist attacks. Whole areas of our towns and cities are no-go zones, especially after dark. Just recently, I read of another spate of burglaries, and there are regular reports of people being mugged and raped. Gangs of teenagers are roaming the streets, and it just isn't safe to go anywhere alone any more. It's all got out of control, but nobody seems to do anything about it. What happened to law and order?

It's a sad fact, but crime happens. Always has done, and always will. And people expect their governments to do something about it. That doesn't seem unreasonable, as one of the first duties of any government is to protect its citizens. The problem is, how do they go about it without becoming too authoritarian or even tyrannical? It's a perennial subject for political debate, this one, especially around election time. One

side claims to be the party of law and order, while the other accuses them of abusing their power. Or one claims to be the champion of liberty, while the other accuses them of being soft on crime.

As you would expect, philosophers are just as divided on the issue as the politicians. And each one has his own recipe for the mix of freedom and security he thinks works best. Coming down on the side of authoritarianism is **Thomas Hobbes**, with his jaundiced view of human nature. He'd look at the sort of news items you've been reading and ask, "Well, what did you expect?" Left to their own devices, he says, that's how people behave. And because they can get away with it, that's what these people are doing in your neighbourhood. If you want something done about it, you have to give somebody the authority to act. That's what you have governments for.

Hobbes would say that the only way to maintain order and to guarantee a degree of security is through the rule of law. Without law, in a state of anarchy, nobody is safe

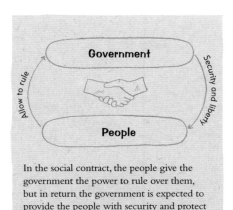

In the social contract, the people give the government the power to rule over them, but in return the government is expected to provide the people with security and protect their liberties.

from the selfishness, greed and brutality of others. So, you appoint a government, which will enact laws forbidding crimes, and a police force to enforce those laws and a justice system to ensure the wrongdoers are punished. You give them the authority, and they will protect you, and the more authority they have the safer you will be.

All you have to do in return for that security is give up some of your liberty. And that's not such a high price to pay, according to Hobbes. Under strong leadership (which he prefers to the term authoritarian), you can walk out of your door knowing that the law will be enforced, keeping the wrongdoers off your streets. In return, you may have to put up with the inconvenience of an intrusive police presence, and some lack of privacy, such as having your correspondence and internet activity monitored. And maybe have to abide by a few laws that you're not so comfortable with, like having to produce identity documents on demand, or not

being able to join certain organizations. Still, if you've got nothing to hide, you've got nothing to fear.

Security and liberty

That's beginning to sound a bit sinister, **John Locke** would say. Surely the deal we make with our governments, the "social contract", is to protect not just our property but our liberty too. We shouldn't just be signing away our rights and handing over authority for the government to tell us what we can and can't do. Governments should be the servants of the people, not their masters, and the system of law should be there as a neutral arbiter to ensure that justice is done. It's got to be more of a two-way relationship – a government can only have legitimate authority when it governs with the consent of the people who are being governed. In that way, we can expect our rights of life, liberty and property to be protected, and to feel both secure and free. Liberty and security are not mutually incompatible, and indeed we should expect our government to provide us with security by the very process of protecting our liberties. You should feel free to walk out of your front door without the fear of attack, but also without the feeling that you're constantly under suspicion.

This kind of political framework, Locke argues, would encourage a more cooperative society, in which everybody feels they have a stake. By establishing a fair social contract, we create a society that respects the rights of all its citizens and encourages cooperation, so that there is less reason for them to turn to crime or violence. This addresses the causes of crime, rather than just the crimes themselves.

Mind you, Locke would add, anybody who is caught breaking the law has by doing so opted out of this arrangement, and forfeits those rights. To discourage this sort of behaviour, Locke advises they should be "destroyed as a lion or tyger, one of those wild savage beasts with whom men can have no society nor security". In other words, the way to deal with crime, to borrow the slogan of Theodore Roosevelt's foreign policy, is to speak softly and carry a big stick.

It's a tricky business, all the same, giving anybody any kind of power. Even Locke recognized that it was necessary, but had to be carefully administered. **John Stuart Mill** felt strongly about it too, and believed that our liberties are too precious to be put at risk. In his opinion, all moral and political philosophy boils down to the idea that everybody has the right to do whatever he or she wants to do, so long as it doesn't harm anybody else, or get in the way of them doing what they want. So, in your case, he'd say that your liberty to walk the streets is being encroached, you are being prevented from doing what you want. So far, so good. Because this is causing you harm, the people responsible, the criminals, terrorists and marauding teenagers, are in the wrong.

But now we hit upon the problem of what should be done with them. Locking them up would be an infringement of their liberty, and any form of punishment would be "causing them harm". So wouldn't that be morally wrong too? Wouldn't that be an abuse of power by the government, the police and the justice system, and done with our authority? Not, says Mill, if you add a second clause to his basic principle of doing no harm: it is morally permissible to exercise power over someone against his will if, and only if, it is done to prevent him from harming somebody else. So you've no need to feel bad when the police come and take away that suspicious-looking character who turns out to have robbed all the houses in your street. Not that you would, of course.

Justice or freedom?

All of that sounds very fair and reasonable, and as English as afternoon tea. For a more passionate analysis of your plight, let's consult a couple of Frenchmen, starting with **Albert Camus**. But don't expect any solace from

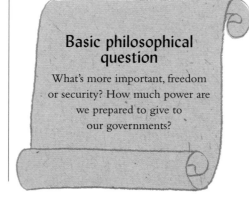

Basic philosophical question
What's more important, freedom or security? How much power are we prepared to give to our governments?

what he has to say, as his reputation for nihilism is legendary. All the same, he makes a fair point when he says that Hobbes hit the nail on the head by saying that if you want justice, you have to give up some freedom. Taken to its extreme, Camus argues, this means that absolute justice demands the suppression of all contradiction, and necessarily denies all freedom. The converse is also true, as absolute freedom makes a mockery of justice. You can't have it both ways. Finding a balance between liberty and security is next to impossible, and in practice the pendulum swings from one side to the other. But perhaps the greatest danger is that security, the safety of the people, is often used as an excuse for tyranny and despotism, and makes the tyrants look as if they're acting out of the goodness of their hearts.

Finally, let's ask **Michel Foucault** for his take on your situation. Like Camus, he would say that your desire for security is being exploited, not exactly by a tyrant, but something very similar, and a lot more insidious. Although the threat of crime and terrorism is real, it is much exaggerated, and it is your perception that is causing your fear rather than any imminent danger. This is because there are people who want you to believe that you're being threatened, want to instil fear in you, so that you will willingly give them the authority to exercise power over you and society. Not necessarily a single tyrant, or even an authoritarian government, but the whole system of power, including the media and other institutions of the establishment.

Foucault warns us that there can never be a total liberation from this kind of power: as it's self-perpetuating, it can be used to create more insecurity, to gain more power. It is being exercised everywhere, and affects us all by changing the way we view the world. The best we can do is try to recognize it wherever we can, and challenge the message of fear. And, if you dare, to step outside your door, Foucault would suggest, and see if you get mugged. The chances are that you won't.

Making a decision

Do you think, as Hobbes does, that a government's job is to maintain law and order? Or would you agree with Locke and Mill that we give government the authority to protect our liberties? That raises Camus's question of how much liberty we are prepared to give up in order to have justice, and whether you're prepared to put up with a tyrant or a police state to feel secure. It may be that you feel that Foucault has it right, that governments and the media exploit people's fears to exercise power over them.

Why do I feel guilty walking past a beggar?

Marx • Singer

You're walking down the street, probably in a hurry to get somewhere, and you see a beggar sitting in a doorway. What's your first reaction? Compassion? No – guilt. And then you either give in to that and drop a coin into her bowl, or resolutely refuse to look her in the eye and carry on past. Then, to assuage your guilt, you tell yourself that she would probably spend the money on drugs or alcohol, or that being a beggar is a lifestyle choice, not a necessity these days. Anyway, you give to charity regularly, don't you? But you still have that nagging guilt…

…and that's probably because deeply ingrained in most cultures is the notion that we all have a responsibility to care for the disadvantaged in society. Nearly every religion makes a point of stressing our duty to give alms, so it's not surprising that it's almost taken for granted that it is a moral duty. Of course, those religious laws came before there were such things as charities or state welfare payments, but the idea that it's sinful not to give to beggars persists.

Karl Marx would argue that beggars used to be a commonplace everywhere in the world, but increasing prosperity in the developed world has meant that we only expect to see them in the poorest countries. And that's because we've gradually forced the state to take responsibility for the disadvantaged. He'd tell you to stop feeling guilty, and start getting angry and active. You noticed the poverty; now look around at all the wealth! That's what governments should be there for: to ensure a just distribution of the wealth of the state, "from each according to their ability, to each according to their needs", so that nobody goes without, and

Basic philosophical question

Do we have a moral duty to help others less fortunate than ourselves? Should aid be a collective or a personal responsibility, or both?

"Give then to the poor; I beg, I advise, I charge, I command you"
St Augustine of Hippo

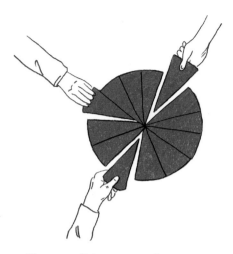

There are sufficient resources for everyone, but they are not distributed fairly.

nobody is reduced to begging or living off the charity of others – in fact, in a decent society, charity shouldn't be necessary. In his lifetime, Marx would tell you, the state only paid lip service to this principle, removing beggars from the streets only to put them in workhouses, forcing them into effective slavery; and fat-cat philanthropists salved their consciences (and got a fair amount of kudos) by spreading their largesse among the poor. But they chose the amount they gave, rather than paying a fair proportion of their wealth to the state to administer where it is most needed. And it's not much better today, even in the richest countries, where there are

still homeless, beggars and people forced to scrape a living in sweatshops or prostitution.

You might agree with Marx that it should be the state's responsibility to look after the most needy in society, or disagree and say that governments should encourage wealth-creators, who would then take responsibility for charitable works. It doesn't matter who *should* be dealing with poverty, the system isn't working, and it seems that Jesus was right when he said, "You will always have the poor among you." So what do you personally do when you come face to face with deprivation? Shrug your shoulders, deny any responsibility and move on?

Emphatically not, if you ask **Peter Singer**. He'd ask you to think of a rather different situation to assess what our individual moral duty is. Imagine, he says, you're walking along the side of a pond and you see a small child drowning. You know the water's only waist-deep, so what do you do? Wade in and rescue her, of course. But you've got your expensive new shoes on! There's no time to waste undoing them, so you'd still wade in. Never mind that the shoes are ruined, that's not as important as that kid's life. Now, would it make any difference to your decision if there were other people there? A policeman, perhaps? Would you walk past hoping one of them would rescue her? It's the policeman's job, right? No, the chances are that you'd still wade in. But what if someone sowed the

"Every day we act in ways that reflect our ethical judgements"
Peter Singer

seeds of doubt in your mind and said the kid was just faking, looking for attention. Would you take that risk?

Almost certainly, you would react the same in each case. But what if he told you about a child drowning in a faraway country, who could be saved by a charitable organization, but they need money to do their work. Would you give the price of a pair of shoes to save a child's life? Or do you think that giving to charities is letting governments off the hook, and providing the aid and services that should be provided by the state? But if they aren't being provided, shouldn't you support the charities if you can?

And when someone tells you that foreign aid paid for by your taxes is being wasted on inefficient schemes and bureaucracy, or worse, pocketed by corrupt regimes, before you complain to your government, ask yourself if you can be sure that's true.

It's only a small part of your taxes, after all. Closer to home, if you and everybody paid their fair share of tax, you wouldn't have the problem of beggars on the street making you feel guilty.

Now, Singer would say, let's not forget that beggar you were talking about. Look at her, and think about the drowning child. You really could spare her the price of a cup of tea. Actually, you could spare the price of a pair of shoes – that would be a fortune to her. So maybe she is pretending, and just doesn't want to work. You can't be sure, and anyway, would it matter if she spent the money you gave her on smokes and drinks? And it really doesn't matter if there are other, richer people than you about, or that she's been abandoned by the social services. It's your individual moral duty to do what you can. Or do you still think it's someone else's responsibility?

Making a decision:

Your guilt is because you feel that the beggar has been let down by the society of which you are a part. The question is whether you think Marx has the right idea, that society as a whole should take responsibility for ensuring nobody ends up on the streets, or whether it should be left to charities and philanthropists. Or you might go along with Singer's argument that we all have a responsibility as individuals to do what we can, by giving to beggars or to aid agencies that can help them.

Why should I do all the household chores? Shouldn't my partner do his fair share too?

Nietzsche • Socrates • de Gouges • Wollstonecroft • Mill • Taylor • De Beauvoir • Anderson • Foucault

Anyone who has lived with a member of the opposite sex knows that the battle of the sexes is not fought on the streets, or even in the workplace, but in the home. Although traditionally men have seen domestic chores as a woman's duty, women are increasingly pointing to the injustice of this arrangement. The argument that men are the ones who go out to work, the breadwinners, no longer washes. It's not just a matter of fairness, though. It's about who wields the power in the household.

This would appear to be a simple question of injustice. There is a certain amount of work that has to be done around the home, but responsibility for it is not equally shared between the couple who occupy that space. Nowadays, women are just about as likely to be going out to work as men, so there are no grounds for the male of the species to claim exemption from the household tasks. And it would be an unusual (and brave) philosopher who tried to put forward an argument to the contrary.

It wasn't always that way, though. Before the 20th century, you'd be hard pushed to find a female philosopher, and the fact that there are indeed two sexes hardly crossed the minds of most of the great (male) thinkers. Except, of course, when it came to domestic chores, and for recreational purposes. **Friedrich Nietzsche** summed up the general philosophical attitude to the female of the species in *Thus Spake Zarathustra*, when he described woman as man's "playmate", whose place was either in the bedroom or the kitchen. The only one who might have given way on the housework issue was **Socrates**, not for any deep philosophical reason, but because his wife Xanthippe really ruled the roost (and allegedly once poured the contents of a chamberpot over her husband's head. Enough said). As for the rest, they would have expected their womenfolk to cater to their requirements, and ensure their comfort and the cleanliness of their home. It wouldn't have crossed their minds that they should do any of that sort of demeaning work, nor that women might be capable (let alone worthy) of anything else.

Socrates showed that men do not always rule the roost.

Changing attitudes

For much of history, women were not so much regarded as second-class citizens, as not considered citizens at all. But things did start to change during the Enlightenment, the so-called Age of Reason, especially following the French Revolution. People started talking about the rights of the citizen, and a couple of brave women brought up the subject of women's rights. Although they didn't mention it explicitly, both **Olympe de Gouges** (1748–93) in her *Declaration of the Rights of Woman and the Female Citizen* and **Mary Wollstonecraft** (1759–97) in *Vindication of the Rights of Woman*, would have come down firmly on the right of a woman to come home from work to find her partner had cleaned, tidied and cooked for her. As you would expect, given their gender.

But it would be interesting to turn to a mid-Victorian English household, that of **John Stuart Mill** and his wife **Harriet Taylor** (1807–58), to see how far attitudes had changed. An ardent proponent of women's rights, Taylor would have insisted on following her own career rather than being chained to the kitchen sink, but, interestingly, her husband would have been happy to comply. Quite apart from the fact that he was a considerate English gentleman, and Britain's leading philosopher, he also campaigned for equal rights for women, even suggesting in Parliament that they should be given the vote. The title of his essay "The Subjection of Women" gives a pretty clear idea of how he viewed the way women were expected to kowtow to their menfolk.

As the movement for women's rights gained momentum, with the fight to get the vote, the battle became a very public one, and to some extent the domestic aspects were overlooked or trivialized. Never mind about who manages the household, the suffragettes might say, what about who runs the country? But with second-wave feminism, after the battle for citizenship had been won, the struggle for true recognition continued on all fronts. Women wanted equality in the workplace, and in the home too. Inspired by **Simone de Beauvoir's** *The Second Sex*, feminist philosophers identified all sorts of ways in which women were still being oppressed. No question which side of the fence they would come down on in the debate over allocation of domestic duties. And this time, men were being forced to take notice, albeit reluctantly. The macho mores of the past were very gradually being eroded, paving the way for the "New Man", the male feminist, who appeared in the late

20th century, and who wore his apron and wielded his vacuum cleaner with pride.

A man's world

Nevertheless, evidence was stacking up that women, despite the progress that had been made, were still getting a raw deal compared to men. Male dominance is so ingrained that it permeates just about every aspect of life and all our ideas about the world. As the American philosopher **Elizabeth S. Anderson** (b. 1959) put it, these ideas "reflect an orientation geared to specifically or typically male interests or male lives". It could have been the household chores she was referring to.

But she was alluding to something more than just housework, and more even than the subjection of one sex by the other. French polymath **Michel Foucault** would look at something as apparently minor as the household duties argument and tell you that it is not simply a domestic dispute, nor even just about the battle of the sexes, but fundamentally a question of the nature of power itself. Power, according to Foucault, is not something that somebody possesses, nor something that can be given or taken, but exists because of the way it is exercised. It's not even about forcing somebody to behave in a certain way; that sort of dominance just encourages resistance. In fact, it is seldom a

"There can never be a total liberation from power, especially in relation to the politics of sexuality"
Judith Butler

> *"God created woman. And boredom did indeed cease from that moment – but many other things ceased as well! Woman was God's second mistake"*
> Friedrich Nietzsche

case of one side actually imposing rules. It's more often a silent battle, in which one side achieves a hegemony.

What, you may ask, does Foucault mean by "hegemony"? Well, it is a form of dominance, and of subjugation, but carries with it the idea that the dominant power has gained the passive consent of the person being subjugated. And the household chores provide an example in microcosm of how this can happen. It has long been the case that men exercise power over women, either overtly by forcing them to stay at home and do the household chores, or more subtly by denying them the opportunity to make a life for themselves outside the home, presenting the situation as a cultural norm.

By a process of attrition, a woman can be made to accept that it is her duty to do the cleaning, tidying, laundry, shopping and cooking. In such a hegemony, there is no need for compulsion in the exercise of power.

But nowadays women, especially the increasing number who have managed to break from the stereotypes, can also exert pressure on their male partners. There is the possibility of resistance, a withdrawing of consent to be oppressed, by a withdrawal of labour. This often follows a similar process of attrition: a man, faced with an untidy, dirty household, no clean clothes and no meal on the table, may be shamed into doing his fair share too, and once the precedent has been established, it becomes the norm.

Making a decision

Of course this depends on your gender...and the majority of philosophers have been men who would sympathize with Nietzsche's idea that women are there to minister to the needs of men. Not all, though, and Socrates, Mill and others would argue for a fairer distribution of the household duties. And if you are a woman, you more than likely wholeheartedly agree with de Gouges, Wollstonecroft, Taylor, de Beauvoir, Anderson and all the feminist philosophers that men should pull their weight in the home, and women should not be subjugated. Whatever your gender, you might agree with Foucault that this issue is a microcosm of the way in which power is exercised by one group over another.

"One is not born a woman, but becomes one"

Simone de Beauvoir

Bibliography

Sources of quotes

Chapter 1

Page 12: Immanuel Kant, *Groundwork of the Metaphysics of Morals* (1785)

Page 14: Hasidic saying, attributed to Rabbi Menachem Mendel of Kotzk (1787–1859)

Page 15: Boethius, *The Consolation of Philosophy* (524 CE)

Page 16: Friedrich Nietzsche, *Twilight of the Idols* (1888)

Page 18: Miguel de Unamuno, *The Tragic Sense of Life* (1913)

Page 19: Roger Scruton, *Modern Philosophy* (1995)

Page 22: Michel de Montaigne, *Essays* Book I (1595)

Page 23: Aristotle (384–322 BCE), *Metaphysics* Book 4

Page 24: René Descartes, *Discourse on the Method* (1637)

Page 26: Jeremy Bentham, *An Introduction to the Principles of Morals and Legislation* (1789)

Page 27: Immanuel Kant, *Foundations of the Metaphysics of Morals* (1785)

Page 29: Immanuel Kant, *Critique of Practical Reason* (1788)

Page 31: Robert Nozick, *Anarchy, State, and Utopia* (1974)

Page 32: Hilary Putnam, *The Many Faces of Realism* (1987)

Page 33: Zhuangzi (*c.*369–286 BCE), *Zhuangzi*, also known as *Nanhua zhenjing* ("The Pure Classic of Nanhua")

Page 34: Plato, the Allegory of the Cave, in *The Republic* Book VII (*c.*380 BCE)

Page 36: Bertrand Russell, *Human Knowledge: Its Scope and Limits* (1948)

Page 38: John Stuart Mill, *On Liberty* (1859)

Page 39: Donatien Alphonse François, Marquis de Sade, *Philosophy in the Bedroom* (1795)

Page 40: John Stuart Mill, *Utilitarianism* (1861)

Page 41: David Hume, *A Treatise of Human Nature* Book 2 (1739–40)

Page 44: Immanuel Kant, *Critique of Judgement* (1790)

Page 45: Aristotle (384–322 BCE), *Metaphysics*

Chapter 2

Page 48: Niccolò Machiavelli, *The Prince* (1513)

Page 49: Paraphrase of Immanuel Kant, in Karl Popper, *The Open Society and Its Enemies* (1945)

Page 50: Friedrich Nietzsche, *The Will to Power* (1888)

Page 52: Friedrich Nietzsche, *Twilight of the Idols* (1888)

Page 54: Arthur Schopenhauer, *The World as Will and Representation,* Volume I (1819,1844,1859)

Page 56: Thomas Hobbes, *Leviathan* (1651)

Page 57: Adam Smith, *The Wealth of Nations* (1776)

Page 59: John Forbes Nash, "Non-cooperative Games", in *Annals of Mathematics*, Volume 54, Number 2 (September 1951)

Page 61: Alan Turing, "Computing Machinery and Intelligence", in *Mind – A Quarterly Review of Psychology and Philosophy*, Volume 59, Number 236 (1950)

Page 63: Gilbert Ryle, *The Concept of Mind* (1949)

Page 65: Jean-Jacques Rousseau, *Confessions of Jean-Jacques Rousseau* (1765–70)

Page 66: Cicero, *De Legibus* (*c.*43 BCE)

Page 67: Robert Nozick, *Anarchy, State, and Utopia* (1974)

Page 69: Adam Smith, *The Wealth of Nations* (1776)

Page 69: Karl Marx, *The Communist Manifesto* (1848)

Chapter 3

Page 75: Thomas Hobbes, *Of Liberty and Necessity* (1654)

Page 76: John Stuart Mill, *On Liberty* (1859)

Page 78: Jeremy Bentham, *An Introduction to the Principles of Morals and Legislation* (1789; 1823)

Page 81: Francis Bacon, *Novum Organum* (1620)

Page 82: Karl Popper, as quoted by Alex Vary in *My Universe: A Transcendent Reality*, Part II (2011)

Page 84: Heraclitus (*c.*540–*c.*480 BCE), as quoted by Plato (c428–c348 BCE) in *Cratylus*

Page 85: Jean-Paul Sartre, *Existentialism Is a Humanism*, lecture (1946)

Page 88: John Locke, *An Essay Concerning Human Understanding (1689)*

Page 89: Arthur Schopenhauer, *On the Freedom of the Will* (1839)

Page 90: Friedrich Nietzsche, *The Dionysian Worldview* (1870)

Page 91: Jeremy Bentham, *An Introduction to the Principles of Morals and Legislation* (1789)

Page 92: Peter Singer, *Animal Liberation* (1975)

Page 94: Sir Isaac Newton (1642–1727), *Irenicum*

Page 95: René Descartes, *Discourse on the Method* (1637)

Page 96: Arthur Schopenhauer, "On the Suffering of the World" (1851)

Page 97: Friedrich Nietzsche, *Beyond Good and Evil* (1886)

Page 98: Confucius (551–479 BCE), *The Analects*

Page 101: Aristotle (384–322 BCE), *Rhetoric*

Page 102: Boethius, *The Consolation of Philosophy* (523 CE)

Bibliography

Page 104: Aristotle, *Nichomachean Ethics* Book II (*c.*325 BCE)

Page 105: Niccolò Machiavelli, *Discourses on Livy* (1517)

Page 106: Friedrich Nietzsche, *Thus Spoke Zarathustra* (1883–91)

Page 107: Bertrand Russell, *A History of Western Philosophy* (1945)

Page 109: Boethius, *The Consolation of Philosophy* (524 CE)

Page 111: Bertrand Russell, *Am I An Atheist Or An Agnostic?* (1947)

Page 113: Socrates (*c.*470–399 BCE), in Plato's *Apology of Socrates* (399–387 BCE)

Page 114: Zeno of Citium (*c.*335–*c.*263 BCE), as quoted in the Epistles of Seneca the Younger (*c.*4 BCE – 65 CE)

Page 115: Epicurus (341–270 BCE), in a letter to Menoeceus

Chapter 4

Page 119: Socrates (*c.*470–399 BCE), quoted by Plato (c428–c348 BCE) in *Apology*

Page 121: Friedrich Nietzsche, *Human, All Too Human* (1878)

Page 123: Aristotle, *On the Parts of Animals* (*c.*350 BCE)

Page 124: Ralph Waldo Emerson, *Nature* (1836)

Page 125: Jean-Jacques Rousseau, *Dialogues: Rousseau, Judge of Jean-Jacques* (1782)

Page 128: Epicurus (341–270 BCE)

Page 129: Diogenes of Sinope (died *c.*320 BCE), quoted by Diogenes Laërtius (flourished 3rd century CE) in *Lives and Opinions of Eminent Philosophers*

Page 132: John Stuart Mill, *Utilitarianism* (1861)

Page 134: Aristotle (384–322 BCE), *Poetics*

Page 136: Arthur Danto, *After the End of Art: Contemporary Art and the Pale of History* (1996)

Page 138: Plato (c428–c348 BCE)

Page 139: William K. Wimsatt and Monroe Beardsley, *The Affective Fallacy* (1949)

Page 140: John Searle, "Reiterating the Differences: A Reply to Derrida" (1977)

Page 142: Arthur Schopenhauer, *The World as Will and Representation* Volume 1 (1818)

Page 143: William K. Wimsatt and Monroe C. Beardsley, "The Intentional Fallacy", *Sewanee Review* (1946)

Page 144: Albert Camus, The Myth of Sisyphus (1942)

Page 145: Arthur Schopenhauer, *The World as Will and Representation* Volume 1 (1818)

Chapter 5

Page 149: Socrates (*c.*470–399 BCE), quoted in Plato's *Euthyphro* (*c.*399–395 BCE)

Page 151: Friedrich Nietzsche, *The Gay Science* (1882)

Page 153: Thomas Hobbes, *Leviathan* (1651)

Page 155: Henry David Thoreau, *Civil Disobedience* (1849)

Page 156: Jean-Jacques Rousseau, *The Social Contract* (1762)

Page 157: Plato, *The Republic* (*c.*380 BCE)

Page 159: Immanuel Kant, *The Metaphysics of Morals* (1797)

Page 160: David Hume, *An Enquiry Concerning Human Understanding* (1748)

Page 162: Adam Smith, *The Wealth of Nations* (1776)

Page 163: David Hume, *Essays, Moral, Political, and Literary* Part I, Essay 6 (1741–2; 1748)

Page 164: Karl Marx, *Capital* Volume II (1893)

Page 165: Henry David Thoreau, *Civil Disobedience* (1849)

Page 167: Confucius (551–479 BCE), *The Analects*

Page 168: Niccolò Machiavelli, *Discourses on Livy* (1517)

Page 169: David Hume, *An Enquiry Concerning Human Understanding* (1748)

Page 172: Voltaire, *The Age of Louis XIV* (1751)

Page 173: Karl Marx, "The Victory of the Counter-Revolution in Vienna", *Neue Rheinische Zeitung*, 7 November 1848

Page 176: John Locke, *Second Treatise of Government* (1689)

Page 178: St Augustine of Hippo (354–430 BCE), Sermon 11 on the New Testament

Page 179: Peter Singer, *The Expanding Circle: Ethics, Evolution, and Moral Progress* (1981)

Page 180: Bertrand Russell, *On Charity* (1932)

Page 183: Judith Butler in *Barcelona Metròpolis* (June–September 2009)

Page 184: Friedrich Nietzsche, *The Antichrist* (1888)

Page 185: Simone de Beauvoir, *The Second Sex* (1949)

Index

Index

Index

Index

Index